Medicare

Other Books in the Current Controversies Series

Medicare

Debra A. Miller, Book Editor

GREENHAVEN PRESS
A part of Gale, Cengage Learning

Detroit • New York • San Francisco • New Haven, Conn • Waterville, Maine • London

Elizabeth Des Chenes, *Director, Publishing Solutions*

For more information, contact:
Greenhaven Press
27500 Drake Rd.
Farmington Hills, MI 48331-3535
Or you can visit our Internet site at gale.cengage.com

For product information and technology assistance, contact us at

Gale Customer Support, 1-800-877-4253
For permission to use material from this text or product, submit all requests online at
www.cengage.com/permissions

Further permissions questions can be emailed to permissionrequest@cengage.com

Articles in Greenhaven Press anthologies are often edited for length to meet page requirements. In addition, original titles of these works are changed to clearly present the main thesis and to explicitly indicate the author's opinion. Every effort is made to ensure that Greenhaven Press accurately reflects the original intent of the authors. Every effort has been made to trace the owners of copyrighted material.

Cover image © Andy Dean Photography/Shutterstock.com.

LIBRARY OF CONGRESS CATALOGING-IN-PUBLICATION DATA

Medicare / Debra A. Miller, book editor.
   p. cm. -- (Current controversies) Summary:"Medicare: This series covers today's most current national and international issues and the most important opinions of the past and present. The purpose of the series is to introduce readers to all sides of contemporary controversies"-- Provided by publisher.
   Includes bibliographical references and index.
   ISBN 978-0-7377-6239-6 (hardback) -- ISBN 978-0-7377-6240-2 (paperback)
   1. Medicare--Juvenile literature. I. Miller, Debra A.
   RA412.3.M423 2012
   368.4'2--dc23

                                                        2012009511

Printed in the United States of America
   1 2 3 4 5   16 15 14 13 12

FD254

Contents

Chapter 1: Are There Serious Problems with Medicare Spending?

Yes: There Are Serious Problems with Medicare Spending

Fraud problems identified a decade ago continue to plague the Medicare program, costing taxpayers an estimated $60 billion a year. Medicare fraud detection contractors are separate from contractors who pay Medicare claims, and often fraud detection contractors do not get accurate information quickly enough. Critics say fraud detection must be built into the payment system so fraudulent claims can be tracked more quickly.

No: There Are No Serious Problems with Medicare Spending

Medicare Is Cheaper than Private Insurance

Judy Dugan

Some politicians propose raising the eligibility age for Medicare from sixty-five to sixty-seven but this is a bad idea. Although Medicare costs are up 400 percent since 1969, the costs of private health insurance have risen 700 percent—nearly twice as much. Medicare costs must be controlled, but it is already better than private plans at cost control.

Medicare Must Be Reformed, but Only to Cover Costs of Additional Beneficiaries

Judy Feder and Nicole Cafarella

Medicare spending accounts for 12 percent of the federal budget, and beginning in 2011 the number of beneficiaries will increase each year as baby boomers begin to turn sixty-five. The Affordable Care Act will help to decrease the per capita costs of Medicare but the growing numbers of older Americans will require greater efficiency in health care across the board as well as more revenue in support of the program.

Medicare Costs Are Rising Much Less than Private Sector Health Costs

Anna Yuhananov

For the fiscal year ending in June 2011, hospital revenues from Medicare rose 2.5 percent per patient while revenue from private insurance rose 7.48 percent. Medicare supporters argue that this is because Medicare is better at negotiating costs with hospitals and other providers than insurance companies. Rising health-care costs are a big problem, not only for Medicare but for everyone.

Chapter 2: Are Doctors Dropping Out of Medicare?

A survey conducted by the Center for Studying Health System Change (HSC) found that close to three-quarters of physicians accepted all or most new Medicare patients in 2008. The rates for Medicaid were slightly lower, with 53 percent of physicians reporting that they were accepting all or most new Medicaid patients.

Controlling Medicare costs necessarily involves lower reimbursement rates for doctors. Yet a recent study showed that even if the average doctor accepted only Medicare patients, his or her yearly income would still be $240,000—an excellent income. If the nation expects to control health-care costs, doctors must make sacrifices to save the health-care system.

Chapter 3: Will the Patient Protection and Affordable Care Act Improve Medicare?

Medicare's hospital coverage is solvent through 2024 and coverage for physician and outpatient services and prescription drugs are not short of funds. In fact, Medicare has led the way in cost containment and thanks in part to changes already adopted as part of recent health-care reforms, Medicare will lead the way in future health-care cost initiatives.

In addition to benefits that help all Americans, the Affordable Care Act will give older Americans several specific new benefits, including drug discounts, free preventative care screenings and benefits, and a free annual wellness exam. More new benefits will unfold each year because the Act's goal is to improve health-care coverage.

The biggest problem with the Affordable Care Act is that it failed to eliminate Medicare's sustainable growth rate (SGR) formula, which determines how much physicians are paid. Even though Congress typically prevents SGR cuts from being implemented, already low Medicare physician payments make it difficult for family practices to remain solvent. The reform law will provide a 10 percent bonus to family doctors, but this is limited and not enough.

Chapter 4: What Steps Should Be Taken to Solve Medicare's Problems?

Neither the Republican voucher idea nor the Democrats' cost-cutting plan will adequately reform Medicare. A better idea is to mandate that Medicare stop paying fee-for-service providers and instead limit the program to non-profit managed care organizations that meet certain criteria. This Medicare reform would keep public health costs low and encourage reforms in private health-care systems, too.

Market-Based Reform Is Necessary for Medicare

James C. Capretta

The proposals for controlling Medicare spending fall into two categories—(1) imposing more government controls and regulation, or (2) encouraging consumers to choose cheaper, better care. The government regulation side has been in control of Medicare for the last thirty years, but health costs have only gone up. It is time to bring more competition and market incentives into the Medicare program by giving a fixed-dollar Medicare contribution to beneficiaries, and making them shop for the best health services and pay for part of that care themselves.

Sharing Costs Is No Way to Fix Medicare

Peter R. Orszag

Republican representative Paul Ryan's plan to cut Medicare spending by shifting it towards consumers will not actually cut Medicare costs. The biggest health-care costs come from expensive treatments for chronic diseases and end-of-life care, and the Ryan plan would not fix this problem. In addition, according to the Congressional Budget Office, the Republican plan would increase total health-care costs per beneficiary because private plans have higher administrative costs and less leverage than Medicare.

Tort Reform Is Needed to Fix Medicare

Richard A. Mathews

The cost of litigation in the United States is astronomical, yet the Seventh Amendment guarantees the right to a civil trial by jury if the amount in dispute exceeds $20. This right should be updated to eliminate trial by jury for litigation demanding less than $50,000. In addition, to save billions spent on defensive patient care, the right to legal recourse of Medicare/Medicaid patients should be limited to instances of gross negligence or fraud.

Foreword

By definition, controversies are "discussions of questions in which opposing opinions clash" (*Webster's Twentieth Century Dictionary Unabridged*). Few would deny that controversies are a pervasive part of the human condition and exist on virtually every level of human enterprise. Controversies transpire between individuals and among groups, within nations and between nations. Controversies supply the grist necessary for progress by providing challenges and challengers to the status quo. They also create atmospheres where strife and warfare can flourish. A world without controversies would be a peaceful world; but it also would be, by and large, static and prosaic.

The Series' Purpose

The purpose of the Current Controversies series is to explore many of the social, political, and economic controversies dominating the national and international scenes today. Titles selected for inclusion in the series are highly focused and specific. For example, from the larger category of criminal justice, Current Controversies deals with specific topics such as police brutality, gun control, white collar crime, and others. The debates in Current Controversies also are presented in a useful, timeless fashion. Articles and book excerpts included in each title are selected if they contribute valuable, long-range ideas to the overall debate. And wherever possible, current information is enhanced with historical documents and other relevant materials. Thus, while individual titles are current in focus, every effort is made to ensure that they will not become quickly outdated. Books in the Current Controversies series will remain important resources for librarians, teachers, and students for many years.

In addition to keeping the titles focused and specific, great care is taken in the editorial format of each book in the series. Book introductions and chapter prefaces are offered to provide background material for readers. Chapters are organized around several key questions that are answered with diverse opinions representing all points on the political spectrum. Materials in each chapter include opinions in which authors clearly disagree as well as alternative opinions in which authors may agree on a broader issue but disagree on the possible solutions. In this way, the content of each volume in Current Controversies mirrors the mosaic of opinions encountered in society. Readers will quickly realize that there are many viable answers to these complex issues. By questioning each author's conclusions, students and casual readers can begin to develop the critical thinking skills so important to evaluating opinionated material.

Current Controversies is also ideal for controlled research. Each anthology in the series is composed of primary sources taken from a wide gamut of informational categories including periodicals, newspapers, books, US and foreign government documents, and the publications of private and public organizations. Readers will find factual support for reports, debates, and research papers covering all areas of important issues. In addition, an annotated table of contents, an index, a book and periodical bibliography, and a list of organizations to contact are included in each book to expedite further research.

Perhaps more than ever before in history, people are confronted with diverse and contradictory information. During the Persian Gulf War, for example, the public was not only treated to minute-to-minute coverage of the war, it was also inundated with critiques of the coverage and countless analyses of the factors motivating US involvement. Being able to sort through the plethora of opinions accompanying today's major issues, and to draw one's own conclusions, can be a complicated and frustrating struggle. It is the editors' hope that Current Controversies will help readers with this struggle.

Introduction

"The [Medicare] program was signed into law on July 30, 1965, by President Lyndon B. Johnson, but it was the culmination of sixty years of efforts to create a program of government health insurance to protect Americans against the ravages of illness, disability, and old age."

Medicare is a nationwide government-run program that provides hospital, medical, and other insurance for older Americans and the disabled. Medicare covers about 47.5 million people (39.6 million aged sixty-five and older and 7.9 million disabled persons) and is funded largely by payroll taxes paid by employees, employers, and the self-employed. With certain exceptions, anyone who reaches age sixty-five, has been a legal resident of the United States for five years, and has adequately paid into the system receives Medicare benefits. The program was signed into law on July 30, 1965, by President Lyndon B. Johnson, but it was the culmination of sixty years of efforts to create a program of government health insurance to protect Americans against the ravages of illness, disability, and old age.

The first battle for public health insurance was waged by the American Association for Labor Legislation (AALL)—a coalition of reformers established in 1906. AALL members included prominent economists, physicians, lawyers, businessmen, professors, labor leaders, politicians, and social workers who were interested in building a social safety net for workers and other Americans. The group first focused on the problem of work-related accidents and succeeded in persuading many states to adopt the first workers' compensation programs. AALL next set out to persuade states to adopt government health insurance programs based on an AALL model bill. Initially, this effort looked promising, winning support from groups such as the American Medical Association (AMA). However, in 1918 and 1919, health-care legislation was defeated in two important states—California and New York—marking the end of the health-care campaign. AALL turned its attention to unemployment insurance and, later, to old-age insurance.

The next push for better health care came in the late 1920s, when a small group of activists convinced several private philanthropic foundations to fund a study of medical issues in the United States. These funds created the Committee on the Costs of Medical Care (CCMC), chaired by Dr. Ray Lyman Wilbur, president of Stanford University and a former president of the AMA. The CCMC spent five years researching medical issues, concluding that various changes should be made to improve the US health-care system. However, only a minority of CCMC members endorsed government-supported health care; the majority believed that Americans should embrace a system of private health insurance—a decision that set the country on a course of private insurance rather than the government-run systems adopted in Europe.

When Franklin D. Roosevelt was elected president in 1932, the time seemed once again ripe for a government health-care proposal. The United States was in the throes of the worst economic disaster in its history—the Great Depression—and the country was coping with massive unemployment, growing poverty, and economic dislocation. As part of his New Deal program, President Roosevelt created a cabinet-level Committee on Economic Security to explore various forms of social insurance to help ordinary Americans. The committee recommended health-care insurance as part of a package of social reforms, but this proposal was met with fierce AMA protests and opposition to any type of government-run health-care insurance. In the end, President Roosevelt felt compelled to drop health insurance from the Social Security Act—a milestone law signed on August 14, 1935, that created old-age insurance (called Social Security) and other social welfare programs. Advocates continued to push for government health insurance thereafter, and Senator Robert F. Wagner of New York introduced a bill in the US Senate to create a Medicare-type program, but ultimately this effort was eclipsed by the outbreak of World War II, as President Roosevelt focused on the war. The Wagner bill failed, many experts believe, because of this lack of presidential support. The president indicated in several speeches that he intended to push for medical insurance once the war ended, but he died in April 1945, before he could keep his promise.

However, the next US president, Harry Truman, was also an enthusiastic supporter of government health insurance, and he included such a proposal in his Fair Deal political platform. After the Japanese surrendered in July 1945, ending the war, President Truman sent a revision of the Wagner bill to Congress. The timing for such legislation at first seemed good, but Truman's health insurance program ultimately failed just like earlier proposals. The reasons for this failure are many: the public's focus on Communism and the Korean War, a trend toward more conservative political ideas, and an effective campaign against Truman's bill by the AMA, all made the passage of government health insurance impossible. The AMA argued that the US system of private health care was already the best in the world and that government control would destroy this free enterprise system and make health care more costly. Truman's government plan also lost support as more and more employers in the United States began adopting private, employer-paid health-care plans, partly because of union demands. When the Republican candidate, Dwight D. Eisenhower, won the presidency in 1952, the cause of government health care for all Americans seemed completely lost.

The next stage of the fight for government health care, therefore, involved the idea of limiting such a program to the elderly and disabled—a population that was rapidly growing in the United States. This group of Americans most badly needed hospital and medical care, yet was having difficulty meeting this need due to rising health-care costs and the fact that many private insurers chose not to insure them, since they were not as profitable as healthier beneficiaries. In 1957, the AFL-CIO—the American Federation of Labor and Congress of Industrial Organizations, a large federation of unions—decided to take on the fight; the group helped to get a bill introduced in Congress for government health insurance for older Americans. Over the next few years, numerous congressional hearings were held, in which various types of health insurance proposals were debated. The election of Democrat John F. Kennedy in the 1960 presidential election, and Kennedy's strong support for a Medicare-type program, created the best chance in decades for such a program to be enacted. The Kennedy administration submitted a draft bill to Congress, and the debate continued, with labor and citizens' groups in favor and the AMA in opposition. When supporters finally pushed the bill for a vote in July 1962, however, it was soundly defeated. An effort to revive the legislation began in late 1963 but was interrupted by the assassination of President Kennedy on November 2 of that year. Ironically, however, Kennedy's death increased public support for his programs, and incoming President Lyndon B. Johnson took advantage of it to push many of Kennedy's ideas through Congress. Medicare became one of these legislative successes; after much congressional wrangling, Medicare legislation was entered into law on July 30, 1965. In a tribute to former president Harry Truman, President Johnson signed the bill into law at Truman's presidential library in Independence, Missouri.

Medicare has grown tremendously since 1965, and today the costs and structure of the Medicare program have become the subject of much political debate. The authors of the viewpoints included in *Current Controversies: Medicare* discuss some of the issues surrounding today's Medicare program, including the level of Medicare spending, whether doctors are leaving the program, whether the Patient Protection and Affordable Care Act will improve Medicare, and what steps should be taken to reform the Medicare program.

CHAPTER 1

Are There Serious Problems with Medicare Spending?

Chapter Preface

Since Medicare was enacted in 1965, the program has expanded to provide most older Americans (and the disabled) with basic health insurance. Shortly before Medicare was introduced, for example, only a little more than half of all Americans sixty-five years old and older had any type of insurance against the costs of hospital care, but by 1970 around 97 percent of older Americans were covered by health insurance, thanks to Medicare. Medicare's coverage has expanded as well; prescription drugs and other benefits have been added to the original package of hospital and doctor/outpatient care. The number of beneficiaries covered by Medicare, too, has grown tremendously as the US population has aged. In 1966, Medicare covered 19.1 million beneficiaries, or about 9.7 percent of the US population, but today the program covers about 47.5 million beneficiaries, or around 14.3 percent of the population. Because of aging baby boomers, Medicare is now expected to make another growth spurt—one that will require it to cover 18.4 percent of the population by 2020. According to most health-care experts, the costs of Medicare have also grown dramatically over the years, today taking up a significant portion of the federal budget.

The modern Medicare program consists of four parts—the original Parts A and B and two new parts, C and D. Medicare Part A pays for inpatient care in hospitals, some short-term care at a skilled-nursing facility or hospice, as well as some home health-care services—subject to an annual deductible of $1,068. After the deductible, Medicare pays everything for hospital stays up to sixty days and part of the costs up to one hundred and fifty days. Medicare Part B helps cover doctor services and outpatient care, plus some preventive services, but generally this help is limited to 80 percent of the Medicare-approved amount for covered services. (Many people purchase private insurance—often referred to as "Medigap" insurance—to pay the remaining 20 percent.) Part C was added to Medicare in 1997 to give Medicare beneficiaries the option to receive their Medicare benefits through private health insurance plans—called Medicare Advantage plans—instead of the government-run Parts A and B. Medicare pays Part C insurers, but Medicare Advantage subscribers typically also pay a monthly premium to cover items not covered by Parts A and B, such as dental care, vision care, and gym memberships. Medicare Part D was added to the program in 2006 to help seniors pay for prescription drugs. Individuals who are eligible for Part A or B are also eligible for Part D, after they enroll in a prescription drug plan or Medicare Part C.

According to the latest statistics from the Center on Budget and Policy Priorities, Medicare and two other federal health programs—Medicaid and the Children's Health Insurance Program (CHIP)—together account for 21 percent of the US budget, or $732 billion. Medicare alone makes up around 14 percent of the budget, or $452 billion. A small part of the Medicare revenues comes from beneficiary premiums— monthly payments for Part B coverage ($99.90 for beneficiaries earning less than $85,000/year or $170,000 for couples in 2012), plus premiums charged to Part A beneficiaries who have not worked the minimum number of quarters to qualify for premium-free Part A coverage. The bulk of Medicare monies, however, is derived from payroll taxes on younger workers and their employers. Essentially, the Medicare program is based on the idea that younger, working Americans are taxed to pay the Medicare costs of older people, so that members of one generation pay the health-care costs of the generation that preceded them. Currently, the payroll tax for employees, called the Federal Insurance Contribution Act (FICA) tax is 7.65 percent of income—6.2 percent for Social Security (Old-Age, Survivors, and Disability Insurance or OASDI) and 1.45 percent for Medicare. Employers withhold the 1.45 percent employee Medicare contribution from employees' paychecks and then match it to create a total Medicare tax of 2.9 percent of income. The self-employed pay the full 2.9 percent of income tax directly to the federal government. This Medicare tax has risen from .35 percent in 1966 to the current rate of 2.9 percent. Beginning in 2013, the 2.9 percent rate will continue for the first $200,000 of income ($250,000 for couples) but will rise to 3.8 percent on income above these levels.

Despite the increases in Medicare taxes, tax revenues do not fully pay for benefits. A recent estimate by the Urban Institute, for example, found that the average single man pays about $55,000 over his lifetime in Medicare taxes but reaps about $161,000 in benefits. The difference is an unfunded Medicare liability that comes out of the general fund of the US federal budget. In addition, Medicare spending is rising rapidly, creating a long-term cost problem for the Medicare system. According to a 2011 report by the government's Medicare trustees, the Medicare Hospital Insurance (HI) fund—which pays for Part A expenses—will be exhausted by 2024 unless action is taken by Congress to raise taxes or otherwise reform the program. The fiscal status of Medicare has recently become a hotly debated political issue, and the authors of viewpoints in this chapter address the basic question of whether there are serious problems with Medicare spending.

Medicare Program Costs Are Not Sustainable

Timothy F. Geithner, Hilda L. Solis, Kathleen Sebelius, Michael J. Astrue, Charles P. Blahous III, and Robert D. Reischauer

Timothy F. Geithner is secretary of the US Treasury; Hilda L. Solis is secretary of the US Department of Labor; Kathleen Sebelius is secretary of the US Department of Health and Human Services; Michael J. Astrue is commissioner of Social Security. They, along with Charles P. Blahous III and Robert D. Reischauer, serve on the Social Security and Medicare Boards of Trustees.

Each year the Trustees of the Social Security and Medicare trust funds report on the current and projected financial status of the two programs. This message summarizes our 2011 Annual Reports.

The financial conditions of the Social Security and Medicare programs remain challenging. Projected long-run program costs for both Medicare and Social Security are not sustainable under currently scheduled financing, and will require legislative modifications if disruptive consequences for beneficiaries and taxpayers are to be avoided.

The long-run financial challenges facing Social Security and Medicare should be addressed soon. If action is taken sooner rather than later, more options and more time will be available to phase in changes so that those affected have adequate time to prepare. Earlier action will also afford elected officials with a greater opportunity to minimize adverse im-

Timothy F. Geithner, Hilda L. Solis, Kathleen Sebelius, Michael J. Astrue, Charles P. Blahous III, and Robert D. Reischauer (Social Security and Medicare Boards of Trustees), "Status of the Social Security and Medicare Programs: A Summary of the 2011 Annual Reports," *Social Security Administration*, May 5, 2011. Reproduced by permission.

pacts on vulnerable populations, including lower-income workers and those who are already substantially dependent on program benefits.

Both Social Security and Medicare, the two largest federal programs, face substantial cost growth in the upcoming decades due to factors that include population aging as well as the growth in expenditures per beneficiary. Through the mid-2030s, due to the large baby-boom generation entering retirement and lower-birth-rate generations entering employment, population aging is the largest single factor contributing to cost growth in the two programs. Thereafter, the continued rapid growth in health care cost per beneficiary becomes the larger factor.

Social Security

Social Security expenditures exceeded the program's non-interest income in 2010 for the first time since 1983. The $49 billion deficit last year (excluding interest income) and $46 billion projected deficit in 2011 are in large part due to the weakened economy and to downward income adjustments that correct for excess payroll tax revenue credited to the trust funds in earlier years. This deficit is expected to shrink to about $20 billion for years 2012–2014 as the economy strengthens. After 2014, cash deficits are expected to grow rapidly as the number of beneficiaries continues to grow at a substantially faster rate than the number of covered workers. Through 2022, the annual cash deficits will be made up by redeeming trust fund assets from the General Fund of the Treasury. Because these redemptions will be less than interest earnings, trust fund balances will continue to grow.

After 2022, trust fund assets will be redeemed in amounts that exceed interest earnings until trust fund reserves are exhausted in 2036, one year earlier than was projected last year. Thereafter, tax income would be sufficient to pay only about three-quarters of scheduled benefits through 2085.

Under current projections, the annual cost of Social Security benefits expressed as a share of workers' taxable wages will grow rapidly from 11-1/2 percent in 2007, the last pre-recession year, to roughly 17 percent in 2035, and will then dip slightly before commencing a slow upward march after 2050. Costs display a slightly different pattern when expressed as a share of GDP [gross domestic product, a measure of the country's total economic output]. Program costs equaled roughly 4.2 percent of GDP in 2007, and are projected to increase gradually to 6.2 percent of GDP in 2035 and then decline to about 6.0 percent of GDP by 2050 and remain at about that level.

The Disability Insurance (DI) program satisfies neither the long-range nor short-range tests for financial adequacy.

The projected 75-year actuarial deficit for the combined Old-Age and Survivors Insurance and Disability Insurance (OASDI) Trust Funds is 2.22 percent of taxable payroll, up from 1.92 percent projected in last year's report. This deficit amounts to 17 percent of tax receipts, and 14 percent of program outlays.

The 0.30 percentage point increase in the OASDI actuarial deficit and the one-year advance in the exhaustion date for the combined trust funds primarily reflects lower estimates for death rates at advanced ages, a slower economic recovery than was assumed last year, and the one-year advance of the valuation period from 2010–2084 to 2011–2085.

While the combined OASDI program continues to fail the long-range test of close actuarial balance, it does satisfy the conditions for short-range financial adequacy. Combined trust fund assets are projected to exceed one year's projected benefit payments for more than ten years, through to 2035. However, the Disability Insurance (DI) program satisfies neither the long-range nor short-range tests for financial adequacy. DI costs have exceeded non-interest income since 2005 and trust fund exhaustion is projected for 2018; thus changes to improve the financial status of the DI program are needed soon.

Medicare Part A Hospital Funding

Relative to the combined Social Security Trust Funds, the Medicare HI Trust Fund [federal hospital insurance trust fund, which pays for Medicare Part A benefits] faces a more immediate funding shortfall, though its longer term financial outlook is better under the assumptions employed in this report.

Medicare costs are projected to grow substantially from approximately 3.6 percent of GDP in 2010 to 5.5 percent of GDP by 2035, and to increase gradually thereafter to about 6.2 percent of GDP by 2085.

Projected long-run program costs for both Medicare and Social Security are not sustainable under currently scheduled financing.

The projected 75-year actuarial deficit in the HI Trust Fund is 0.79 percent of taxable payroll, up from 0.66 percent projected in last year's report. The HI fund fails the test of short-range financial adequacy, as projected assets drop below one year's projected expenditures early in 2011. The fund also continues to fail the long-range test of close actuarial balance. Medicare's HI Trust Fund is expected to pay out more in hospital benefits and other expenditures than it receives in income in all future years. The projected date of HI Trust Fund exhaustion is 2024, five years earlier than estimated in last year's report, at which time dedicated revenues would be sufficient to pay 90 percent of HI costs.

The share of HI expenditures that can be financed with HI dedicated revenues is projected to decline slowly to 75 percent in 2045, and then to rise slowly, reaching 88 percent in

2085. Over 75 years, HI's actuarial imbalance is estimated to be equivalent to 21 percent of tax receipts or 17 percent of program outlays.

The worsening of HI's projected finances is primarily due to lower HI real (inflation-adjusted) non-interest income caused by a slower assumed economic recovery, and by higher HI real costs caused by higher assumed near-term growth in real economy-wide average labor compensation. The resulting increases in HI real deficits are concentrated in the near term, which is why trust fund exhaustion occurs five years earlier than was projected last year despite a relatively modest increase in the 75-year actuarial deficit.

Medicare Part B Doctor/Outpatient and Part D Drug Funding

Part B of Supplementary Medical Insurance (SMI), which pays doctors' bills and other outpatient expenses, and Part D, which provides access to prescription drug coverage, are both projected to remain adequately financed into the indefinite future because current law automatically provides financing each year to meet the next year's expected costs. However, the aging population and rising health care costs will cause SMI costs to grow rapidly from 1.9 percent of GDP in 2010 to approximately 3.4 percent of GDP in 2035 and approximately 4.1 percent of GDP by 2085. Roughly three-quarters of these costs will be financed from general revenues and about one-quarter from premiums paid by beneficiaries. Small amounts of SMI financing are received from special payments by States and from fees on manufacturers and importers of brand-name prescription drugs.

Projected Medicare costs over 75 years are about 25 percent lower because of provisions in the Patient Protection and Affordable Care Act, as amended by the Health Care and Education Reconciliation Act of 2010 (the "Affordable Care Act" or ACA). Most of the ACA-related cost saving is attributable to a reduction in the annual payment updates for most Medicare services (other than physicians' services and drugs) by total economy multifactor productivity growth, which is projected to average 1.1 percent per year. The report notes that the long-term viability of this provision is debatable. In addition, an almost 30-percent reduction in Medicare payment rates for physician services is assumed to be implemented in 2012, notwithstanding experience to the contrary.

The drawdown of Social Security and HI trust fund reserves and the general revenue transfers into SMI will result in mounting pressure on the Federal budget. In fact, pressure is already evident. For the sixth consecutive year, a "Medicare funding warning" is being triggered, signaling that projected non-dedicated sources of revenues—primarily general revenues—will soon account for more than 45 percent of Medicare's outlays. That threshold was in fact breached for the first time in fiscal 2010. A Presidential proposal is required by law in response to the latest warning.

Legislative Correction Needed

Projected long-run program costs for both Medicare and Social Security are not sustainable under currently scheduled financing, and will require legislative corrections if disruptive consequences for beneficiaries and taxpayers are to be avoided.

The financial challenges facing Social Security and Medicare should be addressed soon. If action is taken sooner rather than later, more options and more time will be available to phase in changes so that those affected can adequately prepare.

Medicare Spending Will Likely Grow Even Faster than the Government Projects

Veronique de Rugy

Veronique de Rugy is an economist at the Mercatus Center, a research organization located in Virginia's George Mason University, and a columnist for Reason *magazine.*

Myth: The government's cost projections are reliable.

Fact: They are not. No matter what governmental body does the scoring, it is almost invariably unreliable. . . .

In 1967 long-run forecasts estimated that Medicare would cost about $12 billion by 1990. In reality, it cost more than $98 billion that year. Today it costs $500 billion.

Cost Overruns Common

When it comes to the federal government, massive cost overruns are the rule, not the exception. The $800 billion cost of the war in Iraq dwarfs the $50–60 billion that Mitch Daniels, then director of the Office of Management and Budget, predicted at the outset. In light of these numbers it's interesting to remember that Larry Lindsey, President George W. Bush's economic advisor, was fired for projecting that the war could cost between 1 and 2 percent of GDP [gross domestic product, a measure of the country's total economic output] back in 2002 (roughly between $100 and $200 billion).

Strangely, lawmakers seem to never expect these extra costs even when the excesses take place under their own noses. The Capitol Hill Visitor Center, an ambitious three-floor un-

Veronique de Rugy, "The Facts About the Government's Medicare Cost Projections," Reason.com, June 3, 2011. Copyright © 2011 by Reason Foundation, 3415 S Sepulveda Blvd., Suite 400, Los Angeles, CA 90034, www.reason.com. Reproduced by permission.

derground facility, originally scheduled to open at the end of 2005, was delayed until 2008. The price tag exploded from an original estimate of $265 million in 2000 to a final cost of $621 million.

At the heart of the problem is the massive amount of budget gimmicks, the abuse of rosy scenarios, the emergency spending loopholes, and a lack of fiscal discipline by lawmakers who just can't stop spending the taxpayers' money. . . .

---

*Short-term economic projections are frequently unreli-
able—especially when the projections are done by the
government.*

Federal Debt Projections

[Another good example is the] Congressional Budget Office [CBO] long-term projections of the debt held by the public from 2010 with long-term projections calculated in 2007. In 2007, the CBO projected that the debt held by the public would surpass 60 percent in 2023. Note that this long-term projection incorporated policy changes that were deemed likely at the time. Using the same methodology last year, the CBO projected that the debt will exceed 60 percent of GDP by the end of 2010. In the three years between projections, the debt milestone has accelerated by 13 years. This unforeseen acceleration is worth careful consideration; as the government consumes more credit, less will be available to the private sector.

In other words, even short-term economic projections are frequently unreliable—especially when the projections are done by the government. . . .

Medicare Spending Projections

A more realistic path for Medicare spending . . . [can be calculated by comparing] the long-term projections of Medicare costs under the current law (the 2011 Trustees Report) with the Centers for Medicare and Medicaid Services' Office of the Actuary's alternative projections (2011 Trustees Report Alternative). The latter projections were released as a "best estimate" of future Medicare expenditures to address the "likely understatement of current-law projections."

These projections primarily differ in their assumptions about the plausibility of drastic payment-rate cuts. If such cuts do not materialize, Medicare will cost tens of billions more each year than current law projects.

Furthermore, under the Patient Protection and Affordable Care Act, physician payments are tied to a sustainable growth rate mechanism (SGR), which adjusts repayment rates in order to cap physician-related spending. Since 2001, physicians have been scheduled to receive at least a 5 percent reimbursement cut each year under SGR; and this cut has been overridden by Congress every year except 2002.

In 2012, physician payments are scheduled to decrease by 29.4 percent—an update which is extremely unlikely to occur. So while the Board of Trustees is legally bound to incorporate these cost savings into its projections, the Office of the Actuary has formed a more realistic baseline which incorporates increasing physician repayments into the total cost of Medicare.

Under the current-law baseline, Medicare spending is projected to grow from 3.99 percent of GDP in 2020 to 6.25 percent of GDP in 2080; under the alternative scenario, Medicare spending is projected to grow from 4.31 percent of GDP in 2020 to 10.36 percent of GDP in 2080. In nominal terms, this is a cost underestimation of $2.7 trillion dollars by the year 2080.

Problems Persist with Medicare Fraud Contractors

Kelli Kennedy

Kelli Kennedy is a reporter for the Associated Press, a global news-gathering organization.

Contractors paid tens of millions of taxpayer dollars to detect fraudulent Medicare claims are using inaccurate and inconsistent data that makes it extremely difficult to catch bogus bills submitted by crooks, according to an inspector general's report released Monday.

Medicare's contractor system has morphed into a complicated labyrinth, with one set of contractors paying claims and another combing through those claims in an effort to stop an estimated $60 billion a year in fraud. The U.S. Department of Health and Human Services inspector general's report—obtained by *The Associated Press* before its official release—found repeated problems among the fraud contractors over a decade and systemic failures by federal health officials to adequately supervise them.

Health officials are supposed to look at key criteria to find out whether contractors are effectively doing their job—for instance, how many investigations the contractors initiate. But investigators found that health officials sometimes ignored whether contractors were opening any investigations at all.

The contractors are supposed to detect fraud by checking basic data, such as what type of service was given, how much of it was given and how much it cost. But not all contractors were looking at the same types of data, and some of the information was inaccurate.

Kelli Kennedy, "Problems Persist with Medicare Fraud Contractors," SFGate.com, November 14, 2011. Reproduced by permission of Press Association Incorporated.

The same issues were identified 10 years ago by inspector general investigators, and dozens of reports in the past decade also have found problems. In 2001, acting Inspector General Michael Mangano testified that the Centers for Medicare and Medicaid Services wasn't doing a good job of holding contractors accountable.

"The issues we identified have been problematic for some time and present a serious obstacle" to overseeing the contractors, Inspector General Daniel R. Levinson wrote in Monday's report.

Medicare officials have repeatedly said the latest system of fraud contractors was designed to fix the problems with earlier contractors and allow the agency to better monitor them.

Critics say fraud contractors have been revamped over the years, but nagging problems persist. Investigators found that one contractor referred only two cases of potential fraud to Medicare officials between 2005 and 2008; another did not refer any. But they may have no incentive to refer cases because they are not paid contingency fees for doing so, investigators said. Many experts agree.

"Very few private contractors have financial incentives which are genuinely linked to protection of public funds," said Malcolm Sparrow, a health care fraud expert at Harvard University.

In 2010, inspector general officials testified on Capitol Hill that contractors reviewing fraud in Medicare's prescription drug program also faced serious problems. One contractor didn't receive certain data until nearly one year after being awarded the contract. Once it received the data, key parts were missing or incorrect. Another contractor didn't have access to certain data before its contract ended.

In Monday's report, contractors also said they had difficulty obtaining data they needed and said that daily access to real-time Medicare claims data is critical. One contractor said it eventually had to buy the data from another contractor, which caused a 30-day delay.

The contractors generated only about 100 cases each of potential fraud using the limited data during a nine-month period. Critics say those figures are anemic compared to the billions of dollars of fraud occurring annually.

U.S. Sens. Tom Carper, D-Del., and Tom Coburn, R-Okla., have introduced legislation that would require Medicare officials to share fraud data with law enforcement and contractors, as well as put accuracy requirements into the payment administration contracts.

Medicare officials said they are working diligently to give contractors access to data. They also said the investigation was conducted during early stages of the transition, so many issues have since been addressed. They agreed contractors should have access to data, but the agency has not indicated that improved access has been put in place.

Historically, Medicare has paid claims first and reviewed them later, which worked when most providers were hospitals. But the "pay and chase" method gives criminals weeks of lag time to get paid for fraudulent claims and skip town before authorities catch on.

Critics say separating contractors who pay claims from fraud contractors has created a system where the two are essentially working against each other. Fraud detection must be built into the payment system so contractors can track fraudulent claims as soon as crooks send them in, not days or weeks later, said Kirk Ogrosky, former head of the Justice Department's division that investigates health care fraud.

"By divorcing the job of paying claims from detecting fraud, CMS encourages an ineffective 'pay-and-chase' system," he said.

Medicare Is Cheaper than Private Insurance

Judy Dugan

Judy Dugan is research director for the Foundation for Taxpayer and Consumer Rights, located in Santa Monica, California, and a blogger at Consumer Watchdog, a consumer research website.

Sometimes it takes just a couple of numbers to clarify a huge, complex issue—In this case, what to do about Medicare. Medicare costs are up 400% since 1969—scary, right? But private health insurance premiums in the same period are up 700%—nearly twice as scary.

In today's [June 13, 2011] *New York Times*, economist and columnist Paul Krugman uses these figures to take on a seemingly moderate attempt to reform Medicare, after a plan to do away with direct funding of Medicare (the GOP [Republican] budget plan) died in the Senate. The new plan, from Sen. Joe Lieberman, is to raise the age of eligibility for Medicare from 65 to 67. The plan would toss 65- and 66-year-olds back to the private market to buy health insurance on their own—in the name of "saving" Medicare. But just like the GOP plan to privatize all Medicare, Lieberman's idea fails from the start.

Higher Costs for Private Insurance

Krugman acknowledges that Medicare is a huge and rising cost—up 400%, adjusted for inflation, since its inception in 1969. But what about private insurance? Up 700%:

> So while it's true that Medicare has done an inadequate job of controlling costs, the private sector has done much worse. And if we deny Medicare to 65- and 66-year-olds, we'll be

Judy Dugan, "Private Insurance vs. Medicare: Truth in Numbers," www.Consumerwatch dog.org, June 13, 2011. Reproduced by permission.

forcing them to get private insurance—if they can—that will cost much more than it would have cost to provide the same coverage through Medicare.

By the way, we have direct evidence about the higher costs of private insurance via the Medicare Advantage program, which allows Medicare beneficiaries to get their coverage through the private sector. This was supposed to save money; in fact, the program costs taxpayers substantially more per beneficiary than traditional Medicare.

Krugman cites all the familiar figures from the rest of the developed world, where some mix of public insurance with some private elements manages to cover almost everyone and at a much lower cost than in the United States. But that less-private system of health care has been taken off the table in this country by the private corporate interests who profit from the expensive mess of a health care system we have now.

Medicare needs better cost controls, but it's already cheaper—and better—than private insurance would be for Americans who are 65-plus.

Privatizing Medicare—the Wrong Solution

But further privatizing health care, especially for the elderly, is very far in the wrong direction—even the seemingly moderate proposal by Lieberman to up the Medicare age to 67. From Krugman:

Not every 65- or 66-year-old denied Medicare would be able to get private coverage—in fact, many would find themselves uninsured. So what would these seniors do?

Well, as the health economists Austin Frakt and Aaron Carroll document, right now Americans in their early 60s without health insurance routinely delay needed care, only to become very expensive Medicare recipients once they reach 65.

This pattern would be even stronger and more destructive if Medicare eligibility were delayed. As a result, Mr. Frakt and Mr. Carroll suggest, Medicare spending might actually go up, not down, under Mr. Lieberman's proposal.

These are crazy times in government, when leading politicians see a for-profit industry as the way to cut Medicare spending. Especially when the for-profit industry is driving spending much faster than the government alternative.

And for those who say it's not just about money, that the private market does a better job overall—guess what? Medicare is better on all counts, according to a major 2002 study by the Commonwealth Fund. The study's bottom line: "Medicare outperforms private sector plans in terms of patients' satisfaction with quality of care, access to care, and overall insurance ratings."

So yes, Medicare needs better cost controls, but it's already cheaper—and better—than private insurance would be for Americans who are 65-plus. The real conundrum is how to get the same better deal for the rest of us.

Medicare Must Be Reformed, but Only to Cover Costs of Additional Beneficiaries

Judy Feder and Nicole Cafarella

Judy Feder is a senior fellow at the Center for American Progress, a progressive think tank. Nicole Cafarella is a payment reform project manager and policy analyst at the Center for American Progress.

Concerns about Medicare spending are front and center in discussions of how to rein in our federal budget deficit. That concern is understandable given Medicare's share of the federal budget—at 12 percent and growing. At the same time, Medicare's trustees predict that Medicare's Part A trust fund, which pays primarily for hospital care, will become insolvent—with revenues insufficient to pay full benefit—by 2024.

Whether from a fiscal or a solvency perspective, then, these projections raise real challenges for sustaining the Medicare program. Today 48.5 million people rely on Medicare to make quality health care affordable. In 2035, when Medicare has absorbed the baby boom generation, beneficiaries of the program will number 85.3 million.

Factors Driving Medicare Spending

Serious proposals to address these challenges can only be based on a clear understanding of the underlying facts about what is driving Medicare's cost growth. The two most salient facts are these:

Judy Feder and Nicole Cafarella, "What's Driving Up the Cost of Medicare? Per Capita Costs Will Fall but the Number of Retiring Baby Boomers Will Not," www.american progess.org, June 14, 2011. Copyright © 2011 Center for American Progress. This material was created by the Center for American Progress, www.americanprogress.org.

- The payment changes in the Affordable Care Act enacted last year actually do "bend the cost curve" by bringing the projected growth in Medicare spending per beneficiary well below projected per capita growth in health care spending overall.

- Medicare spending is not just about costs per beneficiary but also about the number of beneficiaries—and this year is when the baby boom generation begins to turn age 65 and becomes eligible for Medicare, adding a million and a half more beneficiaries to Medicare's rolls every year.

Health care spending in general and Medicare in particular have grown faster than the economy.

This means the Medicare program will be doing its part to become more effective and efficient in "per capita" spending, controlling the cost of health care while improving the quality of care, but more revenues will be needed to support the growing numbers of older Americans who are aging into the Medicare program.

Medicare can continue to slow its spending growth through the payment reforms required by the Affordable Care Act. But to achieve a sustainable slowdown will require that all payers—private as well as public—commit to efficiency in health care across the board. This issue brief will demonstrate why extending Medicare's effectiveness in containing costs to the private sector, not turning Medicare into private insurance, is the right way to rein in our nation's health care costs and to reduce the federal budget deficit.

Medicare spending is the product of two components: the dollars spent on each beneficiary and the number of beneficiaries. This decade marks a change in the relative role each plays in driving growth in Medicare spending. So let's look at each aspect of Medicare spending in turn.

The Affordable Care Act's Impact

Although Medicare spending per enrollee has grown more slowly than private health care spending for most of its history, health care spending in general and Medicare in particular have grown faster than the economy. But provisions in the Affordable Care Act to reduce growth in payments to providers such as hospitals, skilled nursing facilities, and home health agencies mean that growth in Medicare per beneficiary spending will fall well below overall growth in health spending per person and well below growth in the economy.

From now until 2019, the last year for which total spending data are available, overall health spending per person is expected to increase at an average annual rate of 5.6 percent. Medicare spending will grow 3 percentage points slower.

More remarkably, Medicare's per beneficiary spending growth of 2.8 percent from 2010 to 2021 is expected to be a full percentage point below growth in per capita gross domestic product, the broadest measure of products and services in our economy. That's a dramatic turnabout from the previous decade. From 2001 to 2010, Medicare per capita spending grew an average of 6.8 percent, or 3.7 percentage points faster than per capita GDP [gross domestic product, a measure of the country's total economic output].

Starting in 2011, Medicare enrollment will increase by a million and a half people every year.

The Baby Boom Generation Effect

At the same time this slowdown occurs, however, the number of enrollees in Medicare begins to rise. The first of the baby boomers become eligible for Medicare in 2011. In contrast to enrollment growth from 2001–2010 (average annual growth in beneficiaries was 1.9 percent or half a million to a million more people each year), enrollment from 2011–2020 is projected to grow by an average of 3 percent per year, or a million and a half more people each year.

What does this mean for overall spending growth? For the first time in Medicare's history, growth in the number of Medicare beneficiaries has become a major factor in driving growth in total Medicare spending. In the 1970s, average annual enrollment growth was 3.4 percent while average annual per capita growth was four times greater (13.4 percent). That was the only decade in which Medicare eligibility was expanded (to include people with disabilities). From 1980 through 2010, average annual enrollment grew at a steady rate just below 2 percent; average annual per capita spending grew four to five times faster.

Morphing Medicare into a private insurance market— the conservative "solution" to rising health care costs— make[s] no sense.

In every decade prior to the one coming up, growth in spending per capita has been the predominant factor in determining how fast overall Medicare spending grows—ranging from four to five times the rate of growth in beneficiaries. In the coming decade, with the baby boomers on the rolls, for the first time the two components will be equal.

The Bottom Line

Over the next two decades, Medicare will welcome the baby boomers born between 1946 and 1964 onto its rolls as they turn age 65. By 2035, 20 percent of the U.S. population will be aged 65 or over, up from 13 percent today. Starting in 2011, Medicare enrollment will increase by a million and a half people every year. Even with efficiencies that slow Medicare cost growth, taking care of a substantially larger older population will simply require spending more.

Recognizing the demographic facts doesn't obviate Medicare's need to spend federal health care dollars effectively and efficiently to slow the growth of health care costs while improving the quality of care for each and every beneficiary. But arguments that efficiency will come from morphing Medicare into a private insurance market—the conservative "solution" to rising health care costs—make no sense. There is simply no evidence that a private marketplace can match Medicare's ability to slow spending growth. With Medicare's per capita cost growth already lower than GDP and projected to diverge increasingly from private health care spending, vouchers for private insurance would actually increase per capita costs.

Building an effective partnership between public and private payers to slow the cost of health care across the economy—not just in Medicare—will take time. But Medicare beneficiaries can't wait.

What does make sense to achieve further per capita spending reduction is to align the private sector with the public sector's commitment to health care payment reform. The Affordable Care Act requires Medicare to find ways to reward better, not just cheaper, care. To make sure that happens, the law sets an annual target for Medicare per capita spending growth and triggers Medicare payment changes if spending projections indicate the target will be breached. To slow the per capita growth rate systemwide, policymakers should enact legislation that modifies the target to apply beyond Medicare to private insurance spending and to trigger all-payer payment reform if the target is breached.

Understanding what's driving Medicare costs makes it clear that Medicare is doing its part to slow growth in spending per beneficiary as the number of beneficiaries begins to increase. But Medicare's payments can deviate only so far from private insurers' payments before health care providers start avoiding Medicare patients or demanding that private insurers make up for Medicare's low rates. The upshot: Measures to further constrain Medicare per capita spending without regard to overall health spending are misguided.

What's needed are measures to assure that all payers—private and public—are partners in payment reform—or legislation that sets limits on systemwide health spending and holds all payers accountable for payment reforms to achieve it. Only a systemwide partnership can effectively slow spending and secure coverage at the same time.

Building an effective partnership between public and private payers to slow the cost of health care across the economy—not just in Medicare—will take time. But Medicare beneficiaries can't wait, and the Medicare trust fund is exhausted in 2024. Arguments that individual retirees themselves can finance the extra spending through Medicare vouchers or other means ignores fundamental realities, among them:

- Medicare benefits are not generous.

- Beneficiaries already pay substantial sums (and shares of income) out of pocket.

- Medicare premiums are already means-tested, with higher-income beneficiaries required to contribute more.

Greater efficiency in per beneficiary spending by the Medicare program will go a long way to ease the burden of paying for a growing elderly population. And bringing private payers into the cost-control system set up by the Affordable Care Act for Medicare will definitely take time and effort. So in the meantime—amid today's debate in Washington about how to rein in the federal budget deficit—policymakers simply have to recognize that Medicare will need more federal revenues to get all the way there.

This is a small price to pay for living up to the nation's commitment to assuring affordable health care to the nation's seniors.

Medicare Costs Are Rising Much Less than Private Sector Health Costs

Anna Yuhananov

Anna Yuhananov is a health and drug policy reporter based in Washington, DC.

Growth in hospital revenue from Medicare patients was roughly one-third the rate seen from patients on private health insurance during the past year, according to data from Standard & Poor's [S&P, a financial rating agency].

Medicare revenue rose 2.5 percent per patient in the year before June [2011], the slowest rate since S&P started keeping track in January 2005, the S&P Healthcare Economic Index showed on Thursday [August 18, 2011]. Revenue for patients on commercial insurance rose 7.48 percent in the year ending in June.

The S&P Healthcare Economic Indices measure the revenue hospitals and other healthcare providers receive for treating each patient under Medicare and commercial insurance programs.

Medicare's Lower Costs

Medicare is the federal health insurance program for the elderly and disabled, with most patients 65 years or older. It has come under heightened public scrutiny as Congress seeks ways to cut government spending, with healthcare costs being one of the biggest contributors.

Defenders of programs like Medicare note that it has done a better job at negotiating down costs with hospitals and other providers than insurance companies, and Thursday's data may bolster that argument.

"In Medicare, the government sets the rules. It's a single payer, which means it's a single market structure," driving costs lower, said David Blitzer, chairman of S&P's Index Committee.

However, Blitzer could not say why Medicare costs were so much lower than those in the private sector this year, and it could depend on how hospitals and physicians calculate costs.

Left unreformed, Medicare, along with Social Security and Medicaid, will devour 100 percent of all tax revenue by 2047.

For example, in times of economic downturn, hospitals may have a greater incentive to seek reimbursement for general costs, such as heating and rent, through private insurers rather than through Medicare, since Medicare rates are lower, he said.

"There may also be some downward rate pressure that may be generated by the government pushing down Medicare costs," Blitzer said.

S&P's Hospital Commercial Index, which calculates hospitals' revenue from private insurers, rose 8.4 percent, versus 1 percent for hospitals' revenue from Medicare.

As a whole, health care revenue rose 5.6 percent in the year ending in June, almost 2 percent slower than the prior year.

Left unreformed, Medicare, along with Social Security and Medicaid, will devour 100 percent of all tax revenue by 2047, according to the nonpartisan Government Accountability Office.

Paul Van de Water, a senior fellow at the Center on Budget and Policy Priorities think-tank who specializes in Medicare and health coverage issues, said the S&P figures are a reminder that high healthcare costs are not just a problem for government.

"In fact, Medicare may be doing better than the private healthcare sector (in limiting costs)," he said.

CHAPTER 2

Are Doctors Dropping Out of Medicare?

Chapter Preface

Medicare critics claim that the fees paid to physicians and other medical providers are far too low, causing some doctors to drop out of Medicare and refuse Medicare patients. Many of these commentators cite Medicare's Sustainable Growth Rate (SGR) payment formula—the system that determines how much Medicare pays physicians—as the prime reason for this problem. The SGR system was created, in part, to help stabilize rising health-care costs in the Medicare program, but critics claim it is not working because Congress regularly prevents the SGR-required cuts from going into effect. Each year, Congress must pass legislation to prevent Medicare physician fees from dropping substantially. Often, this legislation is passed at the last minute before cuts can occur. The result, critics say, is a system full of financial risk and uncertainty for doctors, many of whom would like to continue seeing Medicare patients but worry about whether they will be reimbursed by Medicare at a reasonable rate.

The SGR was enacted by the Balanced Budget Act of 1997 as an amendment to the Social Security Act to help control Medicare spending under Part B for physician services. It replaced an earlier formula, called the Medicare Volume Performance Standard (MVPS). The original goal of the SGR was to ensure that the yearly increase in physician fees for Medicare beneficiaries would not exceed the nation's increase in per capita gross domestic product (GDP)—a measure of the country's per-person economic output. The federal government makes this determination each year, and if Medicare spending for physician fees exceeds the SGR target for that year, then the amounts paid to physicians are supposed to be reduced in the following year in order to keep overall Medicare costs from increasing sharply.

However, Congress has the authority to overrule implementation of SGR cuts to Medicare physician fees, and in recent years politicians have been routinely lobbied by physician groups, such as the American Medical Association (AMA), to do so. Congressional actions to suspend yearly SGR cuts—so-called doc fixes—occurred every year between 2003 and 2011. But since the underlying law was not changed, the SGR cuts accumulated. In 2010, for example, the SGR formula would have required a 21.2 percent reduction in Medicare physician fees. Subsequent congressional action on the SGR was a two-month doc fix that delayed implementation of the SGR until February 29, 2012. In February 2012, the president signed legislation to delay the scheduled cuts until the end of the year. If no action is taken by Congress at that point, and the current doc fix expires at the end of 2012, according to the government's Centers for Medicare and Medicaid Services, physicians will face about a 32 percent reduction in Medicare reimbursement payments.

Physician advocacy groups and many legislators believe that Congress should pass a permanent doc fix to eliminate or replace the SGR formula for Medicare physician fees. The main obstacle is that such action would cost about $300 billion in lost physician fee cuts, and legislators cannot agree on how to offset this cost of cancelling the SGR program. Doctors are also concerned about various other Medicare cuts and cost-control measures mandated by the Patient Protection and Affordable Care Act, the health-care reform law signed by President Barack Obama in March 2010. In addition, the SGR controversy is caught up in the larger debate about the nation's debt and deficit spending and what should be done to control spending on all entitlements, including not only Medicare but also Social Security and other social programs. The question of access to care and whether physicians will respond to Medicare cuts and cost controls by dropping or cutting back on the number of Medicare patients they treat is the focus of the viewpoints in this chapter.

Doctors Are Opting Out of Medicare at an Alarming Rate

Michael Cohn

Michael Cohn is the editor of the website AccountingToday.com.

Doctors have been opting out of the Medicare system at an alarming rate lately as the system goes through a tumultuous year, leaving some accountants' clients in a bind when they suddenly cannot get their medical bills paid.

Doctors' Frustrations with Medicare

At the New York State Society of CPAs' [certified public accountants] health care conference on Tuesday [September 20, 2010], Katherine Dunphy, director of congressional affairs at National Government Services, a major contractor for Medicare administrative services, described this nightmare scenario. While her company is not supposed to deal directly with Medicare patients, it often finds itself on the receiving end of calls anyway. Still, Dunphy noted that many Medicare patients do not take advantage of the appeals process offered by the program.

Dunphy mostly deals with doctor's offices, which are having a hard time keeping up with the rapid changes in Medicare. The system is on its fourth physician fee schedule of the year, thanks to all the uncertainty and changes brought by the health care reform bill. Medicare has become a daunting system for many doctors' offices, and often not one that reimburses doctors quickly or highly.

While 97 percent of doctors still accept Medicare, according to the Center for Medicare and Medicaid Services, problems with Medicare reimbursement rates have frustrated many physicians and their accounts receivable staff. New York State has the highest number of doctors of any state in the country opting out of the system, according to Dunphy: "Every day we're getting calls from doctors who are saying, 'I can't keep up.'" She noted that in some hospitals on Manhattan's East Side, it is difficult to find a doctor in certain practice specialties who accepts Medicare.

The Medicare system is trying to prod doctors into modernizing their practices.

The Medical Society of the State of New York recently announced that 1,100 doctors had left the system, including the society's own president, who is also boycotting private insurance plans.

One of the problems has been with the perennial "doc fix" that Congress needs to pass on an annual basis to keep the Medicare reimbursement rates for doctors from plummeting more than 20 percent. While Congress has proposed making the fix permanent, that seems about as likely as making the alternative minimum tax patch permanent as well. The confusion in Washington over the "doc fix" and changes from the health care reform bill resulted in Medicare claims processing being delayed for an entire month in June, putting doctors in a precarious position waiting for their patients' claims to be paid.

More Medicare Changes Ahead

Still, the Medicare system is trying to prod doctors into modernizing their practices, taking a carrot and stick approach in some instances. Yet despite all of President Obama's talk about the advantages of electronic medical records and other new technologies that the health care reform bill would usher in, Dunphy said she has actually been seeing an increase in the number of paper claims filed through her office. Her office has to use a scanner to process them for Medicare. She is trying to promote the use of electronic claims processing, but when she goes into doctor's offices, she is sometimes asked to help fix the printer so it lines up the paper forms the right way.

Dunphy has been educating doctors about changes in Medicare service coding and the increasing crackdown on Medicare fraud, as the federal government tries to find ways to curb the cost of health care. New York City has seen an uptick in fraud in some specialties such as physical therapy, where one group in Brooklyn was recently found to have bilked Medicare out of about $72 million.

Doctors and their patients need to find out from their accountants about some important changes in Medicare next year. Starting in 2011, claims have to be submitted within 365 days. That goes for appeals against Medicare determinations as well.

"People hold onto their old medical bills," said Dunphy. "Now is the time to get those in. Look at those receivables."

Accountants should also be telling their physician clients about some of the incentives being offered by the federal government to encourage them to modernize. Under the Recovery Act, beginning in 2011, eligible professionals who implement and report meaningful use of electronic health records will be eligible for incentive payments equal to 75 percent of Medicare allowable charges for covered services furnished for a year, up to a maximum payment of $44,000. However, Dunphy cautioned that the electronic medical records system needs to be certified, and physicians also have to be careful that they don't get ripped off by vendors who don't know what they're doing.

Despite the controversy in the past year over the health care reform bill, retirees should be made aware of the potential benefits. That includes the closing of the so-called "donut hole" in Medicare Part D prescription drug coverage, which has resulted in more than a million seniors receiving a $250 rebate check if they managed to reach that coverage gap this year. Seniors will also be able to get a free annual wellness exam starting next year.

Companies too have been applying for subsidies for covering early retirees under the health care bill. Retirees aged 55 to 65 are eligible under the program, and so far 78 companies in New York have applied for the program to help pay the cost of providing health insurance to early retirees.

There is some good news, but also much uncertainty surrounding Medicare. By December 1, a national deficit commission is supposed to report to the White House and Congress on what kinds of changes are needed to get the country's fiscal affairs in order. As one of the largest and fastest-growing federal programs, especially as more Baby Boomers retire, Medicare is likely to be one major item that's going to be spotlighted.

Doctors Are Limiting the Number of Medicare Patients They Accept

Richard Wolf

Richard Wolf is a reporter for USA Today, *an American daily newspaper.*

The number of doctors refusing new Medicare patients because of low government payment rates is setting a new high, just six months before millions of Baby Boomers begin enrolling in the government health care program.

Limiting Medicare Patients

Recent surveys by national and state medical societies have found more doctors limiting Medicare patients, partly because Congress has failed to stop an automatic 21% cut in payments that doctors already regard as too low. The cut went into effect Friday [June 18, 2010], even as the Senate approved a six-month reprieve. The House has approved a different bill.

- The American Academy of Family Physicians says 13% of respondents didn't participate in Medicare last year, up from 8% in 2008 and 6% in 2004.

- The American Osteopathic Association says 15% of its members don't participate in Medicare and 19% don't accept new Medicare patients. If the cut is not reversed, it says, the numbers will double.

- The American Medical Association says 17% of more than 9,000 doctors surveyed restrict the number of Medicare patients in their practice. Among primary care physicians, the rate is 31%.

The federal health insurance program for seniors paid doctors on average 78% of what private insurers paid in 2008.

"Physicians are saying, 'I can't afford to keep losing money,'" says Lori Heim, president of the family doctors' group.

Some U.S. areas already face a shortage of primary care physicians . . . [and] the trend away from Medicare threatens to make it worse.

Access to Primary Care Physicians

The Centers for Medicare and Medicaid Services says 97% of doctors accept Medicare. The agency doesn't know how many have refused to take new Medicare patients, Deputy Administrator Jonathan Blum says. "Medicare beneficiaries have good access to physician services. We do have concerns about access to primary care physicians."

The AARP [formerly known as the American Association of Retired Persons], the nation's largest consumer group representing seniors, is taking notice. Some U.S. areas already face a shortage of primary care physicians. Policy director John Rother says the trend away from Medicare threatens to make it worse.

A Flight from Medicare

States are starting to see a flight from Medicare:

- In Illinois, 18% of doctors restrict the number of Medicare patients in their practice, according to a medical society survey.

- In North Carolina, 117 doctors have opted out of Medicare since January, the state's medical society says.

- In New York, about 1,100 doctors have left Medicare. Even the medical society president isn't taking new Medicare patients.

"I'm making a statement," says Leah McCormack, a New York City dermatologist. "Many physicians are really being forced out of private practice."

Florida has the highest percentage of Medicare patients, and most doctors can't afford to leave the program. But "the level of frustration has been higher this year than I've ever seen it before," says Linda McMullen of the Florida Medical Association.

The Vast Majority of Doctors Still Accept Medicare

Bill Haskell

Bill Haskell has written for Angry Bear, an online financial blog.

Part of the Medicare Sky Falling story is a claim that doctors are refusing to accept new Medicare patients because of low payments. It is common for politicians and pundits to pontificate declaring Medicare is broken. A doctor himself, Wyoming Senator [John] Barrasso made the claim to CNN's Candy Crowley recently.

Sen. John Barrasso mistakenly claimed that "57 percent of doctors don't want new Medicare patients," which isn't true. His own spokeswoman admits he got it wrong.

> "National surveys have put the number who don't take new Medicare patients as low as 14 percent, and a big American Medical Association survey last year showed only 17 percent of all physicians said they were 'restricting' Medicare patients (either taking none, or just some)." . . .

Critics' Claims

The claim is related to the implementation of the Sustainable Growth Rate [SGR] formula which adjusts physician payments whenever the aggregate cost of Medicare exceeds the calculated growth rate. The Sustainable Growth Rate is outside of the ACA [Affordable Care Act, the health care are reform law passed in 2010] and since its inception has only been applied once in 2002. Congress has repeatedly delayed the decreases by applying short term fixes canceling out the planned SGR adjustments in reimbursements. The proposed

2012 budget also contained delays in implementation. The SGR was passed as a method to control the increasing aggregate cost of Medicare without consideration for the number of services provided.

On the other hand, 62% of Primary Care doctors said they would stop taking new Medicare patients if the SGR formula reimbursement cuts were implemented. To increase reimbursements for primary care, the ACA has in it provisions to increase primary care doctors reimbursements and at the same time reduce reimbursements for specialists.

Wrongly identifying Medicare and Medicaid as the leading cause of rising healthcare costs, the House [of Representatives seeks to] . . . balance the . . . budget on the backs of the poor, the elderly, and . . . children.

Another claim by pundits and politicians is Medicare has been outstripping inflation. This has been true for a number of years; but, a more recent trend shows quite the opposite. Here again pundits and politicians have been claiming the reduction in doctors accepting Medicare patients has been the cause of such a decrease in Medicare cost. I believe we have debunked that claim earlier.

Given that rising healthcare costs drive the cost of Medicare, Medicaid, and even commercial insurance; it is outrageous that people would consider cuts in Medicare and Medicaid as a means to control overall healthcare costs or just give up the fight on rising healthcare costs and sacrifice the poor, the children, and the elderly to vouchers and buyer beware.

Medicare's Performance

How has Medicare been performing recently? Maggie Mahar at Health Beat Blog Deadlock Over The Debt, What It Means to You . . . touches upon the planned cuts in Medicare [Speaker of the House of Representatives] John Boehner proposes and lesser cuts offered by President [Barack] Obama as a compromise to break the statement in Washington between the Democrats, the Republicans, and the Tea baggers. Wrongly identifying Medicare and Medicaid as the leading cause of rising healthcare costs, the House under John Boehner has sought to impose severe cuts in the programs which will in effect balance the deficit and budget on the backs of the poor, the elderly, and the children who depend upon Medicare and Medicaid heavily. Medicare and Medicaid are still on the chopping block for cuts under the recent compromise.

In an update to its S&P Healthcare Indices (12 month moving average), [financial rating agency] Standard and Poor's reports Medicare cost trends decreased with costs growing at a rate of 2.64% annually in May [2011]. So, why attack a program whose costs are decreasing and out-performing the Commercial Index (private healthcare) which showed a 7.35% annual cost?

Medicare is dragging down the cost of commercial insurance and acting as a control on overall healthcare costs.

While both the Commercial and Medicare Indexes showed a slight uptick in May of .25 and .16, Medicare has consistently outperformed commercial healthcare insurance in controlling cost. Medicare's performance comes in light of increased healthcare industry costs and a growing baby boomer population. . . .

The Commercial Index (private healthcare) mirrors the growing costs of healthcare in the US. From the May 2010 levels, the Commercial Index reflects a 7.35% increase, Medicare 2.64%, and the composite of both 5.35%. The Medicare Index shows a widening gap between it and the Commercial Index which appears to be occurring from its control of costs. In effect, Medicare is dragging down the cost of commercial insurance and acting as a control on overall healthcare costs.

While hesitant to declare an outright victory and a long term trend in Medicare cost controls, David Blitzer of the S & P Indices in a conversation with Maggie Mahar indicated this is more than just a blip on the screen. He went on to add:

> We tend to get data from the Centers for Medicare and Medicare about 1 to 1 ½ years after the fact; this is why there is a widespread perception that Medicare spending is still rising 2% faster than GDP [gross domestic product, a measure of the country's total economic output]. S&P is giving us more current numbers, and while the S&P index 'is not perfect,' Blitzer says, 'it's good.
>
> While there is waste in Medicare, it is conceivable Medicare costs could be reined in even further through the ACA and enough such so as to match GDP growth and no more. To squeeze cost the ACA will look to the Advantage Programs Insurers, overpayments to Advantage insurers, payments for some preventable errors, annual increases in reimbursements to hospitals, nursing homes and other institutional providers, and with systematic changes to today's healthcare model which rewards providers for doing more than for better outcomes.

Interesting that S&P downgrades the US Credit Rating while at the same time shows proof of entitlement programs driven by the cost of the healthcare industry are decreasing at a faster rate than their commercial counterparts.

Most Doctors Are Standing by Medicare, Medicaid, and Charity Care

Chelsey Ledue

Chelsey Ledue is a contributing editor for Healthcare Finance News, *a health industry newspaper and website that provides coverage of issues that pose financial challenges to health-care providers and payers.*

Almost 75 percent of physicians accepted all or most new Medicare patients last year, according to the Center for Studying Health System Change (HSC) 2008 Health Tracking Physician Survey.

The survey indicates most physicians contracted with managed care plans, while slightly fewer than six in 10 physicians provided charity care in 2008.

"Physicians' clinical decisions affect how up to 90 percent of every healthcare dollar is spent, so understanding how physicians are organized and practice medicine is critical for policy makers, especially as they engage in the most serious discussion of comprehensive healthcare reform in 15 years," said HSC President Paul B. Ginsburg.

Funded by the Robert Wood Johnson Foundation, the 2008 Health Tracking Physician Survey covers a variety of physician and practice dimensions, from basic physician demographic information, practice organization and career satisfaction to insurance acceptance, compensation arrangements and charity care provision. The survey includes responses from more than 4,700 physicians who provide at least 20 hours per week of direct patient care and had a 62 percent response rate.

Chelsey Ledue, "HSC Releases Key Findings from 2008 Health Tracking Physician Survey," Healthcarefinancenews.com, September 8, 2009. Reproduced by permission.

Findings are detailed in "A Snapshot of U.S. Physicians: Key Findings from the 2008 Health Tracking Physician Survey."

In 2008, 59 percent of U.S. physicians reported providing charity care—defined as free or reduced-cost care—to patients in financial need.

They include:

- Nearly one-third of physicians worked in solo or two-physician practices, 15 percent worked in groups of three to five physicians and 19 percent worked in practices of six to 50 physicians.

- More than 80 percent of physicians surveyed worked full time, more than half (53 percent) were 40–55 years old and almost four in 10 have practiced medicine for more than 20 years. Nine in 10 physicians were board certified, and 22 percent received their medical training outside of the United States or Canada. Almost 40 percent were primary care physicians, 35 percent were medical specialists, including psychiatrists, and 26 percent were surgeons, including obstetrician/gynecologists. Also, 56 percent were either full or part owners of their practices, while 44 percent were employees or independent contractors.

- In 2008, 44 percent of physicians reported receiving some form of performance-adjusted salary—such as an adjustment based on productivity. Roughly a quarter indicated payment by fixed salary, and 20 percent received a share of practice revenue. Productivity factors and overall practice financial performance were the most common financial incentives affecting physicians' compensation.

- Fifty-three percent reported their practices were accepting all or most new Medicaid patients, while 28 percent reported accepting no new Medicaid patients. Eighty-seven percent reported their practices were accepting all or most new privately insured patients, and 74 percent reported their practices accept all or most new Medicare patients.

- Eighty-seven percent had managed care contracts in 2008. Compared with physicians with one or more managed care contracts, physicians without managed care contracts were more likely to have practiced for more than 20 years, work fewer than 40 hours per week, lack board certification, work in solo or two-physician practices, live in the western United States and report practicing in a "non-competitive" environment.

- In 2008, 59 percent of U.S. physicians reported providing charity care—defined as free or reduced-cost care—to patients in financial need. On average, physicians who provided charity care provided 9.5 hours of charity care in the month preceding the survey, which amounts to slightly more than 4 percent of their time spent in all medically related activities.

- Almost three-quarters of U.S. physicians were men in 2008. But for physicians under age 40, slightly more than 41 percent were women, signaling how the composition of the physician workforce may change in the future.

Highly Paid Doctors Should Be Willing to Accept Medicare Rates

Nilesh Kalvanaraman

Nilesh Kalvanaraman is a physician with Unity Health Care, a community health center located in Washington, DC.

Whenever I think of our health care system I think of Dr. Frankenstein's monster, assembled from an assortment of parts, trying to find and give love but reviled by all. Short of killing the monster, how do you fix it?

One of the biggest problems with our health care system is the unchecked growth of health care costs. We know that Medicare does a better job of controlling health care costs than private insurers. Along with this comes lower reimbursement rates for doctors which leads to the oft reported phenomenon of doctors not accepting new Medicare patients or dropping out of Medicare altogether.

Every time I read one of these stories I wonder why doctors can't make a living based on their reimbursements. What would happen if we were paid Medicare rates for every patient we see? Would we really lose money or would we just be getting less than what we're getting now? If so, how much less?

Average Medicare Income

I was pleasantly surprised when about a month ago [July 2011] I came across a study looking at just this question: What if every doctor was paid Medicare rates? This study was published in March 2010 by the Urban Institute and the Medical Group Management Association for the Medicare Payment Advisory Commission (MedPAC). It used reported physician

Nilesh Kalvanaraman, "What If Doctors Got Paid Only Medicare Rates?" Doctors for America, August 31, 2011. www.drsforamerica.org. Reproduced by permission.

compensation along with RVUs [relative valve units, used to calculate medicare compensation for doctors] to calculate what annual compensation (take home pay) would be if all services were paid for under Medicare rates. They took into account regional payment differences, practice expenses, and non-RVU based income.

They projected that if the average physician accepted payment based on the Medicare Fee Schedule her annual compensation (her take home pay) would be roughly $240,000. That's sounds like a very nice yearly income. So why do some doctors not like Medicare reimbursement rates? It's because that total represents a 12% loss in income from $272,000.

Medicare Income for Specialty Physicians

Let's look at some more data. Take a look at the annual incomes for the following specialties and think about whether you consider these amounts fair compensations:

- Orthopedics: $457,000

- ENT [Ear, Nose, and Throat]: $380,000

- Neurosurgery: $689,000

- Radiology: $488,000

If we're going to curb health care costs . . . we're going to have to look at not just how doctors get paid but also how much they get paid.

Those look like great incomes to me, and in fact, all four of these incomes would put you in the top 4% of incomes in the U.S. I picked these four because these would be the hardest hit under a universal Medicare payment plan, they all would take over a 20% hit in annual income. Here's what the table looks like with the change in income:

- Orthopedics: $362,000—20.8% from $457,000

- ENT: $282,000—25.6% from $380,000

- Neurosurgery: $462,000—32.8% from $689,000

- Radiology: $389,000—20.2% from $488,000

Lest you think I'm unfairly biased against specialties, here's what will happen to the three primary care fields:

- Family medicine: $169,000—10.6% from $189,000

- Internal medicine: $175,000—7.9% from $190,000

- Pediatrics: $180,000–8.5% from $197,000

An Excellent Income

These are not insignificant drops in income and I'm sympathetic to the idea that this would be a deep hit to doctors, myself included. If we're going to curb health care costs (overall health care costs are rising at an unsustainable rate) we're going to have to look at not just how doctors get paid but also how much they get paid. The point of highlighting this paper is to show that Medicare rates for all, on an absolute level, would provide an excellent income for doctors. It's only because we get paid so much more that Medicare rates seem stingy.

It may be painful but at some point, we as a profession need to recognize that we are getting compensated very well and that we too will have to make sacrifices to maintain the solvency of our health care system. One of our duties in caring for our patients is making sure they can afford the care they need and if that means that I have to drop from the 94th to the 92nd percentile in income, I'm willing to take the hit.

Will the Patient Protection and Affordable Care Act Improve Medicare?

Chapter Preface

As of the end of 2011, the US Congress remained bitterly divided about such questions as how to reduce the federal debt and whether and how to control rising health-care costs in the Medicare program. Another uncertainty that could have a dramatic effect on Medicare involved the US Supreme Court's decision to review the constitutionality of the Patient Protection and Affordable Care Act (PPACA, also called simply the Affordable Care Act or ACA)—the health-care reform law promoted by President Barack Obama and passed by the Congress in 2010. The ACA continues to be controversial, and many Americans have called for its repeal. Numerous lawsuits also have been filed challenging the constitutionality of the ACA, and the US Supreme Court has now agreed to review issues raised in these lawsuits. The Supreme Court's decision could result in part or all of the ACA being declared unconstitutional, including various provisions that made substantive changes to the Medicare program.

Signed by the president on March 23, 2010, the ACA is a sweeping piece of legislation that mandates numerous reforms not only to private health insurance plans but also to the country's main public health insurance programs—Medicare and Medicaid. Along with other changes, the ACA expands coverage for millions of Americans by allowing people with incomes at or below 133% of the federal poverty level (approximately $10,830 for individuals in 2010) to be covered by Medicaid—a public health program similar to Medicare but run by the states for the poor of any age and paid for by federal, state, and local taxes rather than specifically targeted payroll taxes. This provision in the ACA is expected to add twenty to thirty million people to the Medicaid program.

The ACA also changed the Medicare Part D prescription drug benefit. Before the ACA was passed, Medicare beneficiaries faced a gap in coverage known as the donut hole, which burdened them with significant costs. Medicare required beneficiaries to pay the first $310 of prescription drug costs, then Medicare paid 25 percent of costs up to $2,830, but after that point beneficiaries had to pay 100 percent of drug costs until they reached $4,550. The ACA provided seniors in the donut hole with a $250 rebate in 2010 and in 2011 required drug manufacturers to provide a 50 percent discount on name-brand drugs and provided for federal subsidies for generic drugs. By 2020, the ACA was expected to close the donut hole completely, so that Medicare would pay 25 percent of all drug costs after the first $310.

Multiple other changes were made to Medicare by the ACA. For example, one significant provision gives a 10 percent bonus payment to primary care physicians and general surgeons working in certain areas with physician shortages. In addition, the ACA made substantial cuts to the Medicare Advantage plans in Medicare Part C—the private insurance plans available to Medicare beneficiaries—by lowering the payments made to doctors, hospitals, and other medical providers. Yet another significant change made to Medicare is the creation of an Independent Payment Advisory Board (IPAB) that is charged with reducing the rate of growth in Medicare spending. Other important changes seek to create cost savings by encouraging doctors and hospitals to shift from billing for each and every service provided to using value-based billing, which pays for overall care and encourages preventative measures.

Litigation challenging the ACA was filed not only by individuals and organizations but also by twenty-six states. Most of the legal claims in these lawsuits concern the constitutionality of two ACA provisions. The first issue contests the individual mandate—the ACA provision that requires all private persons to purchase health insurance, be covered by a government health program, or pay a tax penalty for choosing not to be insured. Litigants argue that this provision violates the commerce clause of the US Constitution and that the federal government should not be permitted to require the purchase of insurance. The second issue challenges the ACA's Medicaid expansion provision. States claim that this is an unconstitutional intrusion into states' rights because they would have to pay for the additional Medicaid beneficiaries.

If the Supreme Court agrees with either of these arguments, there is a chance that the entire ACA may be repealed because of another legal issue. The ACA, unlike most federal legislation, does not contain a severability clause—a clause that provides for the rest of a law to be retained even if one part is struck down by the courts. In the absence of such a clause, litigants argue that the entire health reform law would be effectively repealed if any part is found to be constitutionally defective. These questions will be the subject of oral argument, which is scheduled for March 2012, and legal experts anticipate that the Supreme Court will likely rule by June 2012. The authors of viewpoints included in this chapter discuss the various ways that the ACA changes Medicare and debate whether these changes are an improvement to the Medicare system.

Editor note: On June 28, 2012, the US Supreme Court issued its ruling on the ACA, upholding the individual mandate but finding it is unconstitutional for the federal government to withold Medicaid funding for states that refuse to expand their Medicaid programs as the ACA directs. Although the full ramifications of the Court's decision are yet to unfold, many commentators believe that the Court's ruling on the Medicaid issue will take away the federal government's ability to enforce a Medicaid expansion and seriously threaten the ACA's goal of universal health coverage.

The Affordable Care Act Has Improved Medicare's Financial Outlook

Paul N. Van De Water

Paul N. Van De Water is a senior fellow at the Center on Budget and Policy Priorities, an organization that focuses on fiscal policy issues affecting low- and middle-income Americans.

Claims by some policymakers that the Medicare program is nearing "bankruptcy" are misleading. Although Medicare faces major financing challenges, the program is not on the verge of bankruptcy or ceasing to operate. Such charges represent misunderstanding (or misrepresentation) of Medicare's finances.

Medicare's financing challenges would be significantly greater without the health reform law (the Affordable Care Act, or ACA), which substantially improved the program's financial outlook. Repealing the Affordable Care Act, a course of action promoted by some who simultaneously claim that the program is approaching "bankruptcy," would make Medicare's financial situation much worse.

Medicare Is Far from Bankrupt

The 2011 report of Medicare's trustees finds that Medicare's Hospital insurance (HI) trust fund will remain solvent—that is, able to pay 100 percent of the costs of the hospital insurance coverage that Medicare provides—through 2024; at that point, the payroll taxes and other revenue deposited in the trust fund will still be sufficient to pay 80 percent of Medicare hospital insurance costs. (The Medicare hospital insurance program is considered insolvent when revenues and trust fund balances will not cover 100 percent of projected costs.) Over the next 75 years, revenue will cover an average of 83 percent of Medicare's hospital insurance costs. This shortfall will need to be closed through the provision of additional revenues, program changes that slow the growth in costs, or most likely both. But the Medicare hospital insurance will not run out of all financial resources and cease to operate after 2024, as the "bankruptcy" term may suggest.

The 2024 date does not apply to Medicare coverage for physician and outpatient costs or to the Medicare prescription drug benefit; these parts of Medicare do not face insolvency and cannot run short of funds. These parts of Medicare are financed through the program's Supplementary Medical Insurance (SMI) trust fund, which consists of two separate accounts—one for Medicare Part B, which pays for physician and other outpatient health services, and one for Part D, which pays for outpatient prescription drugs. Premiums for Part B and Part D are set each year at levels that cover 25 percent of costs; general revenues pay the remaining 75 percent of costs. The trustees' report does not project that these parts of Medicare will become insolvent at any point—because they can't. The SMI trust fund always has sufficient financing to cover Part B and Part D costs, because the beneficiary premiums and general revenue contributions are specifically set at levels to assure this is the case. SMI cannot go "bankrupt."

Nonetheless, Medicare faces serious financing challenges in order to make the Hospital Insurance trust fund solvent over the long term and to reduce unsustainable federal budget deficits that are driven in part by Medicare's rising costs. Major reforms in health care payment and delivery will be essential throughout the U.S. health care system, and Medicare will need to play an important role in leading the way to those reforms. A first step, however, should be to "do not harm"—that is, not make Medicare's financing challenges even greater. Repealing the Affordable Care Act would do exactly that.

Impact of the ACA

The Affordable Care Act has significantly improved Medicare's long-term financial outlook. Under the trustees' main projection, the Medicare hospital insurance program faces a shortfall over the next 75 years equal to 0.79 percent of taxable payroll—that is, 0.79 percent of the total amount of earnings that will be subject to the Medicare payroll tax over this period. The Medicare actuary estimates that if health reform were repealed, HI's long-term shortfall would increase from 0.79 percent to 3.89 percent of taxable payroll (see figure). Under that analysis, health reform has reduced the size of HI's shortfall by four-fifths. In the absence of the ACA, the Medicare hospital insurance program would become insolvent eight years earlier, in 2016, and the costs of SMI would be significantly higher and rise more rapidly in the years ahead.

Since 1990, changes in the law, the economy, and other factors have brought the projected year of Medicare HI insolvency as close as four years away or pushed it as far as 28 years into the future.

These projections underscore the importance of successfully implementing the cost-control provisions in the Affordable Care Act. White history shows that most major Medicare savings measures have been implemented as scheduled, the Medicare actuary has expressed concern that some of the ACA's savings provisions may not be sustainable. The actuary urges reliance instead on an "illustrative alternative" projection for Medicare, which assumes that only 60 percent of the ACA's Medicare savings will actually be achieved in the long run. Under this alternative projection, the projected insolvency date of the Hospital Insurance trust fund remains at 2024, but the 75-year shortfall in the fund would rise to 2.15 percent of payroll, about 2 3/4 times higher than the trustees' official estimate. This still is a dramatic improvement, however, over the outlook *without* the Affordable Care Act.

Arbitrary 45 Percent General-Revenue Threshold Bears No Relationship to Medicare's Financial Health

The Medicare Modernization Act of 2003 (P.L. 108-173) requires the trustees to issue a "Medicare funding warning" when the overall share of Medicare's financing that comes from general revenue (for all parts of Medicare combined) is projected to exceed 45 percent. The trustees project that this level will be exceeded in 2011 and 2012. The 45-percent level, however, is an arbitrary benchmark that is unrelated to the program's financial health.

Phasing out traditional Medicare and replacing it with private health insurance . . . would represent a big step in the wrong direction.

By design, Parts B and D of Medicare are supposed to be financed in large part with general revenues. That at least 45 percent of Medicare will be financed with general revenues is no more a problem than that 100 percent of defense, education, or most other federal programs is financed with general revenues.

The trustees' latest projections, issued in May [2011], are broadly in line with those that the trustees have issued for some time. They do not represent a striking change in Medicare's finances. Since 1990, changes in the law, the economy, and other factors have brought the projected year of Medicare HI insolvency as close as four years away or pushed it as far as 28 years into the future. The latest projection falls near the middle of that spectrum. Trustees' reports have been projecting impending insolvency for four decades, but Medicare benefits have always been paid because Congress has taken steps to keep spending and resources in balance in the near term. In contrast to Social Security, which has had no major changes in law since 1983, the rapid evolution of the health care system has required frequent adjustments to Medicare, a pattern that is certain to continue.

Long-Term Challenges

Despite the financial improvements the Affordable Care Act makes, Medicare continues to face substantial long-term financial challenges, stemming from the aging of the population and the continued rise in costs throughout the U.S. health care system. The projected increase in long-term Medicare costs also contributes heavily to the bleak federal fiscal outlook. It is essential that policymakers take further substantial steps to curb the growth of health costs throughout the U.S. health care system as we learn more about how to do so effectively in both public programs and private-sector health care. The Medicare research and pilot projects that the ACA establishes should yield important lessons.

In the near term—before these efforts bear fruit—it will be difficult to achieve big additional reductions in Medicare expenditures (although some more modest savings should be achievable), without shifting substantial costs to beneficiaries or greatly reducing payments to providers, either of which would likely endanger access to care for low- and moderate-income beneficiaries. Extending the life of the HI trust fund will almost certainly require *both* reductions in projected HI expenditures *and increases in HI revenues.*

Phasing out traditional Medicare and replacing it with private health insurance, as the House-passed budget resolution would do, would represent a big step in the wrong direction. It would *increase* total health care spending attributable to Medicare beneficiaries—the beneficiaries' share plus the government's share—by upwards of 40 percent. The Congressional Budget Office (CBO) estimates that in 2022 (the first year the new arrangement would be in effect), the plan would cause total health spending attributable to the average 65-year-old Medicare beneficiary to increase from $14,750 to $20,500. The plan would also reduce the federal government's contribution to cover those costs. As a result, it would massively shift costs to the beneficiaries—that is, the elderly and people with disabilities. According to CBO, the average 65-year-old beneficiary's out-of-pocket costs would more than double, from $6,150 a year under a continuation of traditional Medicare to $12,500 under the House plan.

Traditional Medicare—rather than private health insurance—has been the leader in instituting various reforms in the health care payment system to improve efficiency and constrain costs. These include the prospective payment system for hospitals and Medicare's fee schedule for physicians. Partly because of its record of innovation, Medicare has outperformed private insurance in holding down the growth of health costs. Between 1970 and 2009, Medicare spending per enrollee grew by an average of 1 percentage point less each year than comparable private health insurance premiums.

Health reform envisions that Medicare will continue to lead the way in efforts to slow health care costs while improving the quality of care. By eliminating traditional Medicare, the House-passed budget plan would discard the opportunity to use the program to promote cost reduction throughout the health care system. This makes it all the more important that policymakers and the American public not be driven into adopting such a radical proposal by misleading claims that Medicare is on the verge of "bankruptcy,"

Better Medicare, and More

Herald Tribune

The Herald Tribune *is a daily newspaper located in Sarasota, Florida.*

Medicare gets better all the time. That's good news for America's seniors—and bad news for opponents of national health-care reform.

As the annual enrollment period for Medicare begins Saturday, seniors can look forward to more benefits, thanks to the Affordable Care Act, ridiculed by critics as "Obamacare." Those benefits include:

- Drug-price discounts of up to 50 percent for those who reach the Medicare prescription plan's coverage gap—the "donut hole."

- Requiring insurers to fully pay, with no deductibles or co-payments, for numerous screenings and other preventive care such as mammograms, colonoscopies and vaccinations.

- A free annual "wellness exam."

These Medicare benefits are in addition to benefits under the health-care law that help Americans in general, such as:

- Preventing insurers from denying coverage because of pre-existing conditions—protecting children now and all Americans by 2014.

- Requiring insurers to cover young adults on their parents' plan up to age 26.

- Capping policyholders' out-of-pocket expenses.

"Better Medicare, and More," *Herald Tribune*, October 14, 2011. Heraldtribune.com. Reproduced by permission.

More benefits will come on line every year, with the goals of vastly improving coverage for the insured and providing affordable coverage for tens of millions of Americans who now lack insurance.

If President Barack Obama's opponents in Congress and on the campaign trail want to follow through on their threats to repeal the health-care law, they'll have their work cut out. Medicare recipients and middle-class families—the majority of the voting public—would throw a fit, and rightly so.

These benefits were put in place by law because private insurers would not provide them otherwise. Americans will be in no hurry to return to the inadequate and more costly coverage of the past.

Congress [may] face the controversial choice of either canceling many of the law's most important benefits or finding a new way to fund them.

Of course, the U.S. Supreme Court could force the issue. Both the Obama administration and several Republican state attorneys general have asked the court to rule next year on a constitutional challenge to the health-care law.

Florida is among 26 states in which Republican officials have sued to invalidate the Affordable Care Act as an unconstitutional intrusion on states' and individuals' rights.

One of the main concerns is the law's mandate that, by 2014, all Americans either have health insurance or pay a tax penalty.

The mandate is the means by which some of the more expensive, and popular, elements of the plan—such as required coverage of pre-existing conditions—will be paid for.

Without the mandate, Congress would face the controversial choice of either canceling many of the law's most important benefits or finding a new way to fund them.

Would that mean a new tax? An expansion of Medicare to all citizens? A new entitlement?

We suspect that many of "Obamacare's" critics secretly hope the Supreme Court upholds the law. And that would be good news for everyone.

Medicare Is Stronger Because of the Affordable Care Act

Barbara Kennelly

Barbara Kennelly is a former congresswoman and the current president and CEO of the National Committee to Preserve Social Security and Medicare, a membership organization that works to protect and ensure the financial security, health, and well-being of older Americans.

When the Affordable Care Act [ACA] became law last March [2010], critics predicted doom for the seniors and people with disabilities who rely on Medicare. They said that coverage would disappear, benefits would be cut, and death panels were on their way—none of which was true. But these lies scared many seniors about the law before it was explained to them.

Now, one year later, as the implementation of the law moves forward, Medicare is still sound—it's stronger than it was before the law was passed—and millions of people with Medicare are benefitting from the law.

The ACA's Improvements for Medicare

Medicare has gotten serious about cracking down on waste, fraud, and abuse. Last year, the [Barack] Obama administration announced it had recovered $4 billion in Medicare fraud. And the Affordable Care Act provides tools to crack down even further.

The Affordable Care Act specifically says that Medicare's guaranteed benefits—hospital care, doctors' services, home health services, drug coverage, and more—are protected. Ben-

Barbara Kennelly, "Medicare and the Affordable Care Act: Keep Moving Forward," Thehill.com, March 23, 2011. Copyright © 2011 Capitol Hill Publishing Corp. Reproduced by permission.

efits are as good as ever—better, in fact. Prescription drugs are more affordable. This year the nearly 4 million beneficiaries who fall into the prescription drug "doughnut hole" will receive discounts on their drugs. These discounts will increase over the next few years until the doughnut hole is closed.

The Affordable Care Act encourages beneficiaries to get the care they need before they get sick. Now, the more than 44 million people with Medicare can get an annual wellness visit or needed screenings for diabetes or cancers without having to pay a co-pay. Early detection and treatment not only saves money but it saves lives.

Repealing the Affordable Care Act . . . would undo . . . fraud-fighting tools, coverage in the doughnut hole, free preventive care, better coordinated care, and the chance to stay in your own home.

The new law ends Medicare overpayments to insurance companies and rewards those that provide high quality care. But as these changes are phasing in starting this year, beneficiaries still have a wide range of plans to choose from.

States have new options to let seniors and people with disabilities stay in their homes rather than having to move to a nursing home when they need help. And in the coming years, thanks to the new law, Medicare will lead the way to better coordinated patient care that should improve the quality of care while reducing costs.

Threats to the ACA

But there is a threat out there. The new leadership of the House of Representatives has dedicated itself to repealing the Affordable Care Act. This would undo all of these improvements. Fraud-fighting tools, coverage in the doughnut hole, free preventive care, better coordinated care, and the chance to stay in your own home would all be gone.

Even worse is their alternative. Some proposals call for increasing out-of-pocket costs for beneficiaries—something the Affordable Care Act does not do. Representative Paul Ryan, chairman of the House Budget Committee, has a more detailed plan he calls a "roadmap." He calls for jaw-dropping cuts to the program, including raising the eligibility age to 69, slashing Medicare over time by 76 percent, and replacing the program with a cash voucher that would shift most of the cost of health care to individuals. This plan would be devastating both to current beneficiaries and to today's working families who are counting on the Medicare program they pay into to protect them from unaffordable health care costs when they retire.

Representative Ryan leads the House committee responsible for producing a budget. But his roadmap leads us backwards to a period when our most vulnerable were forced to choose between health care costs and other necessities like food and shelter. We reject this vision, and we hope Congress does too. A year ago, we passed the Affordable Care Act to strengthen and improve Medicare for current and future generations. Let's keep moving forward on that path.

The Affordable Care Act Will Not Control Health-Care Costs

Paige Winfield Cunningham

Paige Winfield Cunningham is a reporter for The Washington Times, *a daily newspaper published in Washington, DC.*

Despite President [Barack] Obama's promises to rein in health care costs as part of his reform bill, health spending nationwide is expected to rise more than if the sweeping legislation had never become law.

The ACA's Impact on Health Spending

Total spending is projected to grow annually by 5.8 percent under Mr. Obama's Affordable Care Act [ACA], according to a 10-year forecast by the Centers for Medicare and Medicaid Services [CMS] released Thursday [July 28, 2011]. Without the ACA, spending would grow at a slightly slower rate of 5.7 percent annually.

CMS officials attributed the growth to an expansion of the insured population. Under the plan, an estimated 23 million Americans are expected to obtain insurance in 2014, largely through state-based exchanges and expanded Medicaid eligibility.

The federal government is projected to spend 20 percent more on Medicaid, while spending on private health insurance is expected to rise by 9.4 percent.

The projections came as the legal challenges to the health care bill finally reached the U.S. Supreme Court. In a filing Wednesday [July 27, 2011], the Thomas More Law Center asked the justices to strike down the law, appealing a lower-court ruling that Congress has the authority to require Americans to buy health insurance.

But the projections also gave Republicans—who uniformly opposed the legislation—an opportunity to remind Mr. Obama of the emphasis he put on cutting back health care costs. While trying to sell his health care plan in 2009, Mr. Obama frequently stressed "bending the cost curve."

New provisions will save money for the health care system, even if today's report doesn't credit these strategies with reducing costs.

"Simply put, this report states the obvious, that Americans have known for more than a year—the $2.6 trillion law only makes the fundamental problem of skyrocketing health care costs worse," said Sen. Orrin G. Hatch, Utah Republican and ranking member of the Senate Finance Committee.

The Administration's Response

In a blog post responding to the report, White House Deputy Chief of Staff Nancy-Ann DeParle said the recent growth rates to which the study is unfavorably comparing the ACA's costs have been historically low. National health spending grew by 3.9 percent last year, she said, while growth is typically closer to 6 percent.

The bottom line is that more Americans will get coverage and save money, and health expenditure growth will remain virtually the same, Mrs. DeParle said.

"The Affordable Care Act creates changes to the health care system that typically don't show up on an accounting table," she said. "We know these new provisions will save money for the health care system, even if today's report doesn't credit these strategies with reducing costs."

A Long Way to Go

Health care costs have been rising faster than inflation for years, threatening to eat up an ever-greater share of the federal budget and private-sector spending. Expenditures in the U.S. reached $2.6 trillion in 2010—more than three times the $714 billion spent in 1990—and made up 17.6 percent of the gross domestic product.

As health care spending accelerates over the next few years, the portion paid by the government will grow as well. While federal, state and local governments' estimated share of total health spending was 45 percent in 2010, it is expected to near 50 percent by 2020.

And because those newly insured will be younger and healthier on average, they are expected to visit doctors and use prescription drugs more than visiting hospitals—resulting in slower growth of spending on hospitals than on physician services and prescription drugs.

But even as the ACA will shift around some spending within the health care system, it doesn't fundamentally fix the skyrocketing cost of health care, said Bob Bixby, executive director of the Concord Coalition, a nonprofit focused on eliminating federal budget deficits.

"We went into the health care debate last year with the idea we had to slow the growth of health care costs, and so this report indicates that we haven't done that—that we still have a long way to go," Mr. Bixby said.

The Affordable Care Act Failed to Create Physician Payment Stability

Lee Gross

Lee Gross is a family doctor who shares a medical practice with another family physician in Florida.

Some family doctors say they're staying in Medicare and accepting new Medicare patients because, philosophically, it's the right thing to do. But after participating in Medicare for several years, I've developed a different perspective. I think keeping my practice open is the right thing to do—for my community, as well as for me. Unfortunately, my practice may fold if we stay in Medicare.

I practice in Florida with another family physician. We're exactly what most family physicians used to be—small-business owners in an independent practice.

We stopped accepting new Medicare patients this past January, a gut-wrenching but necessary step. We plan to stop participating in Medicare by the end of this year or the next, and we're likely to opt out of Medicare altogether.

Here's why.

Health Reform and Russian Roulette

Although the AAFP [American Association of Family Physicians] threw its support behind the recently passed health reform bill, I think the bill was ill-conceived in many ways. The biggest tragedy is that the bill didn't eliminate Medicare's sustainable growth rate, or SGR, formula and institute a new formula to create payment stability.

Physicians have been playing Russian roulette with the SGR for years. Before this year, Congress always stepped in to stop SGR-dictated cuts before they started. Even so, Medicare payments became increasingly inadequate, making it hard to keep a practice solvent, much less to make changes to become a patient-centered medical home.

This year [2010] has been even worse. Congress allowed the disastrous 21.3 percent pay cut to go into effect June 1, finally rescinding it a few weeks later and giving us a 2.2 percent increase—but only until Nov. 30. Have you noticed that Nov. 30 is *after* the next election? How convenient for Congress!

Legislators need to step up and push payment reform through.

If Congress lets the 21.3 percent pay cut return after Nov. 30, it will be the death knell for many practices. The typical primary care practice has 60 percent overhead, so there's 40 cents on the dollar to take home at the end of the day. The 21.3 percent pay cut would take away about 20 cents of those 40 cents. I don't know any doctor who can absorb a 50 percent decrease in income and not face some unanswerable repercussions.

Congress might instead continue the 2.2 percent increase after Nov. 30, but Medicare pay still would be inadequate.

Some help will come from the new health reform law, which provides a 10 percent primary care bonus beginning in 2011. Unfortunately, the bonus is only for those who meet certain requirements, only for certain types of claims and only for five years. Furthermore, a 10 percent bonus on top of the possible 21.3 percent pay cut would still equal a disaster, just not of such epic proportions.

The bottom line is that legislators need to step up and push payment reform through, but I'm not optimistic, given their track record.

Unilateral Changes, Unending Hassles

Medicare's penchant for making unilateral changes—and not for the better—is another reason why we're getting out of Medicare as soon as we can.

Our practice won't continue in a system that mandates what we can and can't do in the exam room for strictly financial reasons.

Here's a perfect example. A few years ago, we decided to offer stress tests to detect heart disease. Since we didn't have all the equipment, we and several other doctors rented space in an existing facility and went there once a week to perform the tests.

But Medicare changed the rules so that this violated the Stark laws [which govern physician self-referral, when a doctor sends a patient to a facility in which he or she has a financial interest]. Instead, the facility had to buy mobile equipment, and the technicians had to lug it to our office once a week.

Last January, Medicare changed its rules again. Since the technicians weren't our full-time employees, Medicare decreed that their costs had to be passed through with no profit to us—and we couldn't charge for office space or other costs. We would lose money on every single test. Therefore, the most profitable thing we did with our treadmill in recent months was to sell it. Unfortunately, all of the technicians were out of a job.

Medicare didn't change the rules because of quality concerns. They did it under the guise of eliminating fraud and waste, but I think they changed the rules because they were spending too much money on stress tests. In a discreet form of rationing, we have lost our best way to detect the leading cause of death in the nation. Our practice won't continue in a system that mandates what we can and can't do in the exam room for strictly financial reasons.

There are many other frustrating aspects of Medicare involvement, ranging from the silly bullet points we need in our charts to keep from being audited to the numerous pages of regulations we must wade through to learn how to qualify for "meaningful use" incentives. I can't wait to be done with it all!

Beyond Leaving Medicare

As we reduce our Medicare involvement, we are working to shore up our practice with more commercial payers. We hope to get Medicare to a low enough percentage of our patient base that we won't go out of business if we stop taking Medicare entirely.

However, since all insurers eventually follow Medicare, the problems with Medicare will still haunt us. The only sure way to get out of Medicare's shadow is to stop relying on third-party payers altogether. I frankly think that might be necessary for family medicine to survive.

Millions of formerly uninsured people will need access to family physicians as the provisions of the health reform law go into effect. What will America do if most of our practices go broke and close in the face of this need? I hope other family physicians will consider getting out from under Medicare as we are. If our practice in Florida can do it and survive, maybe your practice can, too.

The ACA's Medicare Cost-Cutting Board Will Limit Access to Health Care and Stifle Medical Innovation

Douglas Holtz-Eakin

Douglas Holtz-Eakin is a former advisor to the presidential campaign of Republican senator John McCain and president of American Action Forum, a conservative policy institute that promotes a smaller federal government.

In this written statement, I hope to make the following points:

- The Independent Payment Advisory Board (IPAB) is a dramatic policy error that will fail to deliver meaningful reform to the Medicare program.

- The IPAB is likely to exacerbate existing reimbursement problems that already limit access to care for Medicare beneficiaries.

- The IPAB will tend to stifle U.S. led medical innovation in the medical device, pharmaceutical, biotechnology, and mobile health industries.

- If left unaddressed, the Medicare *status quo* and the IPAB will pose a danger to the fiscal health of the federal government, the U.S. economy, and Medicare beneficiaries.

Let me discuss each in turn.

Douglas Holtz-Eakin, "Testimony Before the United States House of Representatives, Committee on the Budget," budget.house.gov, July 12, 2011.

The IPAB Is a Dramatic Policy Error

The creation of the Independent Payment Advisory Board is possibly the most dangerous aspect of the Patient Protection and Affordable Care Act [ACA]. It should be repealed immediately.

This appointed panel will be tasked with cutting Medicare spending, but its poor design will prove ineffective in bending the cost curve, and instead will lead to restricted patients' access and stifled innovation. Four design elements stand-out as especially troublesome.

First, the board is prohibited from recommending changes that would reduce payments to certain providers before 2020, especially hospitals. Because of directives written into the law, reductions achieved by the IPAB between 2013 and 2020 are likely to be limited primarily to Medicare Advantage (23 percent of total Medicare Expenditures), to the Part D prescription drug program (11 percent), and to skilled nursing facility services (5 percent). That means that reductions will have to come from segments that together represent less than half of overall Medicare spending.

The Independent Payment Advisory Board is at best a band-aid on out-of-control Medicare spending and at its worst a threat to physician autonomy and patient choice.

Second, [if] IPAB's cuts have to be achieved in one-year periods there will be an enhanced focus on reducing reimbursements at the expense of longer-run quality improvements or preventive programs. In this way IPAB could actually discourage rather than encourage a focus on quality improvement.

Third, IPAB is effectively unaccountable. In practice, the law makes it almost impossible for Congress to reject or modify IPAB's decisions, even if those decisions override existing laws and protections that Congress passed. It's not really an advisory body, despite its name. The system is set up so that IPAB, rather than Congress and HHS acting under Congress' authority, makes the policy choices about Medicare.

All of this suggests that IPAB is a potent mechanism for undesirable policy. The Independent Payment Advisory Board is at best a band-aid on out-of-control Medicare spending and at its worst a threat to physician autonomy and patient choice.

Saving Medicare from ruin requires nothing short of total and comprehensive reform. Adding in more cuts to a broken system does not make it any less broken. The IPAB proposals will be short-term fixes and cuts. We need long-term thinking and long-term solutions. We need to move the focus from merely containing costs to focus on how to get the most value for our health care dollars. . . .

The IPAB Is Likely to Exacerbate Existing Reimbursement Problems

If Medicare's provider reimbursements are drastically reduced the market will react in accord with the basic laws of economics. Providers will have three options: to close up shop, to refuse Medicare patients, or to shift the costs onto the other patients. None of these options help our healthcare system operate more effectively or more efficiently.

IPAB introduces further uncertainty into physician reimbursement and is likely to force more physicians to begin making difficult Medicare practice decisions.

Today, Medicare coverage no longer guarantees access to care. Increasingly seniors enrolled in the Medicare program face barriers to accessing primary care physicians as well as medical and surgical specialists. The *New York Times,*

Bloomberg News, and *Houston Chronicle* are among many newspapers reporting that doctors are opting out of Medicare at an alarming rate. For example, the Mayo Clinic, praised by President [Barack] Obama and the IPAB's architects, will stop accepting Medicare patients at its primary-care clinics in Arizona.

The physician access problem stems from Medicare's below-cost reimbursement rates and the uncertainty surrounding the Medicare sustainable growth rate (SGR) formula for physician payments. IPAB introduces further uncertainty into physician reimbursement and is likely to force more physicians to begin making difficult Medicare practice decisions. . . .

The Affordable Care Act substantially increases the cost of innovation.

The last time a major payment reduction loomed . . . , 11.8 percent of physicians stopped accepting new Medicare patients, 29.5 percent reduced the number of appointments for new Medicare patients, 15.5 percent reduced the number of appointments for current Medicare patients, and 1.1 percent of physicians decided to stop treating Medicare patients altogether.

Recognizing the increased payment uncertainty, physician practices have started to reshape their practice patterns. Moving forward 67.2 percent of physician practices are considering limiting the number of new Medicare patients, 49.5 percent are considering the option of refusing new Medicare patients, 56.3 are contemplating whether to reduce the number of appointments for current Medicare patients, and 27.5 percent are debating whether to cease treating all Medicare patients.

Medicare's status quo is fraying the nation's social safety net. The IPAB will only make the net fray more quickly. . . .

The IPAB Will Stifle U.S.-Led
Medical Innovation

By statute, IPAB cannot directly alter Medicare benefits. Instead, the more likely threat to patients is that the IPAB will be forced to limit payments for medical services. In the process, it will effectively determine that patients should have coverage for one particular treatment option but not another, or must pay much more for one of the treatment options.

This is especially troubling because it may choose to disproportionately focus on expensive new treatments. New medicines for conditions like Alzheimer's or Parkinson's will likely have rapid cost growth, especially early after their introduction. That will make them targets because the IPAB is directed to focus on areas of "excess cost growth." Worse, because about one-half of spending is off limits until after 2020, there will be a disproportionate and uneven application of IPAB's scrutiny and payment initiatives.

U.S. medical innovation leadership is dependent on whether the regulatory environment nurtures growth or suppresses innovation. The Affordable Care Act substantially increases the cost of innovation and the IPAB creates a level of uncertainty that will likely drive away venture capital investment in start-up firms and research and development investments from established firms. . . .

Medicare and the IPAB Pose
a Danger to the Fiscal Health
of the Federal Government

Medicare as we know it is financially unsustainable. The reality is that the combination of payroll taxes and premiums do not come close to covering the outlays of the program. . . . In 2010 Medicare required nearly $280 billion in general revenue transfers to meet its cash outlays of $523 billion. As program costs escalate, the shortfalls will continue to grow and reach a projected cash-flow deficit of over $600 billion in 2020.

These shortfalls are at the heart of past deficit and projected future debt accumulation. . . . Between 1996 and 2010, cumulative Medicare cash-flow deficits totaled just over $2 trillion, or 22 percent of the federal debt in the hands of the public. Including the interest cost on those Medicare deficits means that the program is responsible for 23 percent of the total debt accumulation to date.

Going forward, the situation is even worse. By 2020, the cumulative cash-flow deficits of 6.2 trillion will constitute 35 percent of the debt accumulation. Again, appropriately attributing the program its share of the interest costs raises this to 37 percent.

Viewed in isolation, Medicare is a fiscal nightmare that must change course. When combined with other budgetary stresses, it contributes to a dangerous fiscal future for the United States.

The federal government faces enormous budgetary difficulties, largely due to long-term pension, health, and other spending promises coupled with recent programmatic expansions. The core, long-term issue has been outlined in successive versions of the Congressional Budget Office's (CBO's) *Long-Term Budget Outlook*. In broad terms, over the next 30 ycars, the inexorable dynamics of current law will raise federal outlays from an historic norm of about 20 percent of Gross Domestic Product (GDP) [a measure of the country's total economic output] to anywhere from 30 to 40 percent of GDP.

This depiction of the federal budgetary future and its diagnosis and prescription has all remained unchanged for at least a decade. Despite this, action (in the right direction) has yet to be seen.

In the past several years, the outlook has worsened significantly.

Over the next ten years, according to the Congressional Budget Office's (CBO's) analysis of the President's Budgetary Proposals for Fiscal Year 2012, the deficit will never fall below

$740 billion. Ten years from now, in 2021, the deficit will be nearly 5 percent of GDP, roughly $1.15 trillion, of which over $900 billion will be devoted to servicing debt on previous borrowing.

As a result of the spending binge, in 2021 public debt will have more than doubled from its 2008 level to 90 percent of GDP and will continue its upward trajectory.

A U.S. Fiscal Crisis

A United States fiscal crisis is now a threatening reality. It wasn't always so, even though—as noted above—the Congressional Budget Office has long published a pessimistic *Long-Term Budget Outlook*. Despite these gloomy forecasts, nobody seemed to care. Bond markets were quiescent. Voters were indifferent. And politicians were positively in denial that the "spend now, worry later" era would ever end.

Those days have passed. Now Greece, Portugal, Spain, Ireland, and even Britain are under the scrutiny of skeptical financial markets. And there are signs that the U.S. is next, as each of the major rating agencies have publicized heightened scrutiny of the United States. What happened?

The only actions taken thus far have made matters worse.

First, the U.S. frittered away its lead time. It was widely recognized that the crunch would only arrive when the baby boomers began to retire. Guess what? The very first official baby boomer already chose to retire early at age 62, and the number of retirees will rise as the years progress. Crunch time has arrived and nothing was done in the interim to solve the basic spending problem.

Second, the events of the financial crisis and recession used up the federal government's cushion. In 2008, debt outstanding was only 40 percent of GDP. Already it is over 60 percent and rising rapidly.

Third, active steps continue to make the problem worse. The Affordable Care Act "reform" adds two new entitlement programs for insurance subsidies and long-term care insurance without fixing the existing problems in Social Security, Medicare, and Medicaid.

Financial markets no longer can comfort themselves with the fact that the United States has time and flexibility to get its fiscal act together. Time passed, wiggle room vanished, and the only actions taken thus far have made matters worse.

As noted above, in 2020 public debt will have more than doubled from its 2008 level to 90 percent of GDP and will continue its upward trajectory. Traditionally, a debt-to-GDP ratio of 90 percent or more is associated with the risk of a sovereign debt crisis.

Perhaps even more troubling, much of this borrowing comes from international lending sources, including sovereign lenders like China that do not share our core values.

For Main Street America, the "bad news" version of the fiscal crisis would occur when international lenders revolt over the outlook for debt and cut off U.S. access to international credit. In an eerie reprise of the recent financial crisis, the credit freeze would drag down business activity and household spending. The resulting deep recession would be exacerbated by the inability of the federal government's automatic stabilizers—unemployment insurance, lower taxes, etc.—to operate freely.

Worse, the crisis would arrive without the U.S. having fixed the fundamental problems. Getting spending under control in a crisis will be much more painful than a thoughtful, pro-active approach. In a crisis, there will be a greater pressure to resort to damaging tax increases. The upshot will be a threat to the ability of the United States to bequeath to future generations a standard of living greater than experienced at the present.

Future generations will find their freedoms diminished as well. The ability of the United States to project its values around the globe is fundamentally dependent upon its large, robust economy. Its diminished state will have security repercussions, as will the need to negotiate with less-than-friendly international lenders.

Some will argue that it is unrealistic to anticipate a cataclysmic financial market upheaval for the United States. Perhaps so. But an alternative future that simply skirts the major crisis would likely entail piecemeal revenue increases and spending cuts—just enough to keep an explosion from occurring. Under this "good news" version, the debt would continue to edge northward—perhaps at times slowed by modest and ineffectual "reforms"—and borrowing costs in the United States would remain elevated.

Profitable innovation and investment will flow elsewhere in the global economy. As U.S. productivity growth suffers, wage growth stagnates, and standards of living stall. With little economic advancement prior to tax, and a very large tax burden from the debt, the next generation will inherit a standard of living inferior to that bequeathed to this one.

Chapter 4

What Steps Should Be Taken to Solve Medicare's Problems?

Chapter Preface

Historically, with the exception of Medicare/Medicaid and the Veterans Administration (VA) program for US military veterans, the US health-care system has been characterized by a system of private health-care insurance, purchased either by employers or individuals from private health insurance companies, with health care provided by private doctors and hospitals. During the recent debate about health-care reform, many health advocates lobbied the US Congress to adopt a public, government-run health-care program similar to Medicare that would cover all Americans—an idea often called the public option or Medicare for all. Some commentators continue to argue that expanding Medicare to everyone in the United States would help contain costs by spreading the risk by insuring both healthy and unhealthy subscribers and allowing for government containment of drug prices and services. This idea has been criticized as socialism, however, and was soundly rejected by legislators in favor of the Patient Protection and Affordable Care Act (Affordable Care Act or ACA)—a program of expanded health care based on the current system of private health insurance for most Americans (plus Medicare/Medicaid for the elderly, disabled, and poor). Yet most other developed countries have embraced some form of public health care, funded and run by the government, to cover most or all of their people—so-called universal public coverage.

In Europe, for example, most countries have adopted near-universal government-run health insurance programs, but with many variations. The health-care system used in Britain, for example, is an example of truly socialized medicine. Under the country's National Health Service (NHS), health care is provided to everyone by the national government and is funded by taxpayers, with no private insurers involved. The government owns the hospitals, pays the doctors, and buys all prescriptions. Medical treatment is a public benefit for everyone, and no one has to pay out-of-pocket for any health care. At the same time, Britain also has a small private health-care insurance system, which offers better hospital amenities to those who can afford it. The British health system has been compared to the US veterans' health-care program, which is run by the US Department of Veterans Affairs. Many health experts consider this system to be highly cost-efficient, largely because administrative costs are very low and because doctors and other providers are paid a set fee for each patient, regardless of how many office visits or tests are required. This arrangement differs from the US system, in which doctors are paid a fee for each visit with a patient and each test performed, under both private insurance and Medicare.

Another model of public health care is found in Germany. It is closer to the current US system because it uses private health-care providers and insurers. Also like the US system, it is financed by employers and employees; employees pay a monthly insurance premium, and employers pay the rest. The key difference from the American system, however, is that the amount each German employee pays for health insurance is based on his or her income. In addition, unlike the US system, health insurance companies in the German public program must cover everyone and are not permitted to make a profit, and health-care costs are tightly controlled by government regulation of medical services and fees. Germany also has a private, for-profit health-care system, but it can only be used by self-employed individuals, civil servants, and those who earn a large income and choose to opt out of the public system. All German insurers, however, are very heavily regulated by the government, so insurers cannot raise rates after subscribers get sick or as they get older. Other advantages of the German system are that benefits are generous; children are covered for free until they are 18 years old, and the government pays for health coverage if Germans lose their jobs.

A third type of health-care system, used in Canada, is a combination of the British and German models. This system is similar to the US Medicare program because it is funded by income and sales taxes, administered by the government, with services provided by private doctors and private, mostly non-profit hospitals. The system covers all Canadians regardless of pre-existing conditions or income, with no copayments or deductibles, but prescription drugs are typically covered only for the elderly and the poor. Yet drug prices are typically very low for everyone else because the government negotiates prices with drug suppliers. Unlike the US system, Canada's system is not employer-based, and private insurers are limited to covering benefits not offered by the public plan, such as covering costs for routine dentistry, prescription drugs, auto accidents, care while traveling abroad, cosmetic procedures, and private hospital rooms.

No country's health-care system is perfect, however. European systems, for example, have often been criticized for a lack of competition among providers, limited choice of doctors, and long waits for medical services. Even in Canada, the wait for nonurgent medical procedures can be quite long. And all countries are facing the challenge of rising health-care costs and whether and how to limit medical services to those that are most affordable and effective. What these examples of foreign health-care systems offer is a wealth of ideas that could potentially be incorporated into the US system—both the Medicare program and the private insurance market—to help control costs and improve care. The authors of the viewpoints in this chapter discuss a range of other ideas concerning how the US Medicare system might be reformed.

Medicare's Physician Payment System Must Be Replaced

Stuart Guterman

Stuart Guterman is vice president for payment and system reform at the Commonwealth Fund, a private research and advocacy foundation established to promote a better health-care system for Americans, including low-income people, the uninsured, minorities, young children, and the elderly. He is also the executive director of the fund's Commission on a High Performance Health System.

Medicare physician fees are scheduled to be reduced by 27.4 percent on January 1 [2012], unless Congress acts to override that reduction or eliminate the sustainable growth rate (SGR) mechanism that is used to determine the annual update. For nearly a decade, Congress has continued to "kick the can down the road" by temporarily overriding the physician fee cuts that were mandated by the SGR, rather than taking the difficult but necessary step of repealing and replacing the SGR.

The Medicare Dilemma

In considering how to deal with Medicare physician payments, Congress faces a major dilemma:

- Medicare spending is rising at a rate that threatens the program's continued ability to fulfill its mission and contributes to the projected growth of federal spending; but

Stuart Guterman, "Medicare Physician Payment: It's Time for Real Reform," The Commonwealth Fund, November 3, 2011. Commonwealthfund.org. Reproduced by permission.

- The SGR mechanism, which is intended to address that spending growth, produces annual reductions in physician fees that are equally difficult to accept, threatening to distort Medicare payment rates and hamper Medicare beneficiaries' access to care.

This dilemma arises from the underlying mismatch between the primary cause of rising Medicare spending, which is the volume and intensity of services provided, and the fact that the SGR can address rising spending only by reducing the fees that physicians receive for each service they provide.

Replacing the SGR

Congress has been reluctant to let the increasingly larger cuts mandated by the SGR take effect, but has been equally reluctant to eliminate the mechanism that produces those cuts, for fear that it would cause an even steeper increase in Medicare spending. Indeed, the Congressional Budget Office (CBO) estimates that eliminating the SGR and replacing it even with a 10-year freeze in Medicare physician fees would cost upwards of $300 billion.

The high fees paid for physician services in the U.S. contribute significantly to the discrepancy between health spending in this country and the rest of the world.

There are, however, strong arguments for replacing the SGR mechanism:

- It reduces payment rates across-the-board—every service, every specialty, every geographic area—regardless of performance;

- It maintains current incentives for each physician to increase the volume and intensity of services;

- It does not address the undervaluation of primary care services in the physician fee schedule;

- It has failed to control spending growth: in 2002, although physician fees were cut by 4.8 percent, physician spending per Medicare beneficiary rose by 5.2 percent, and from 2003 through 2005, although fees rose by only 1.4 to 1.5 percent each year, spending per beneficiary rose by almost 9 percent per year;

- It has led to increasing gaps between Medicare and private payment rates;

- It has undermined the credibility of the Medicare program with physicians; and

- It does not provide incentives to improve the quality, appropriateness, or coordination of care.

We need to start paying for what we want by rewarding providers for more coordinated, effective, and efficient care.

Physicians' Fees Are Important

To be sure, how much we pay physicians is a critically important issue. We currently spend 50 percent more of our economic resources on health care than any other country and, as the National Scorecard recently released by the Commonwealth Fund's Commission on a High Performance Health System indicates, we often don't receive care that is of concomitantly high quality. Further, there is increasing evidence that the high fees paid for physician services in the U.S. contribute significantly to the discrepancy between health spending in this country and the rest of the world. The large deficits the federal government is running, and is projected to run into the future, only underscore the need to address health spending now.

Yet to make the most appropriate decisions, it's critical to determine how to pay physicians—and other providers—so that the Medicare program gets the best care possible for its beneficiaries. And these issues do not just apply to Medicare: CBO analysis indicates that the major factor driving the long-term growth in federal health spending is rising health care costs per person, which applies throughout our system. High health care costs put pressure on state and local finances, inflate the costs of American businesses, and hinder households' efforts to stay afloat in the face of an economic downturn and rising health insurance premiums and out-of-pocket costs. We therefore must focus not only on federal health spending but also on the underlying cost of care—both public and private—throughout the health sector, or we risk dowsing the flames without really putting out the fire.

We get what we pay for in our health system: an emphasis on the volume of services and complex and high-cost procedures rather than patients' needs. We need to start paying for what we want by rewarding providers for more coordinated, effective, and efficient care. But it's hard to offer effective rewards for better care if the baseline is a 27 percent across-the-board cut in fees, which hits all physicians regardless of the appropriateness, effectiveness, or cost of the care they provide or its impact on the health of the patient.

The Need for Fundamental Payment Reform

What we need is more fundamental payment reform, including measures that:

- Address the chronic underpayment for primary care services;

- Establish accountable care organizations that focus on improving the quality and reducing the cost of patient care rather than producing more services; and

- Encourage development of other innovations in payment, organization, and delivery that would move from fee-for-service payment to more comprehensive payment approaches, such as:

- refining and expanding the patient-centered medical home and other models that enhance the role of primary care and encourage better coordination across providers and settings; and

- bundled payments for acute and post-acute care episodes.

The Affordable Care Act includes provisions that aim to achieve each of these goals, and the challenge falls to us to implement these reforms effectively to improve the performance of our health system.

Payment methods can be adjusted to encourage and reward increasing levels of accountability.

Merely offering alternative models of payment is not enough. We need to make sure that it is no longer rewarding to remain in an unfettered fee-for-service payment environment—and that alternative arrangements are sufficiently attractive. One approach would be to partially or fully exempt providers who participate in alternative models of health care organization, delivery, and financing from any payment cuts that are imposed as part of the response to the immediate need to reduce spending. At the same time, efforts must continue not just to cut fee-for-service payments but also to improve them, because it will take time to make the transition from the current system and because how we pay now will serve as the basis for what comes next.

In changing how we pay for health care, we must recognize the diverse array of organizational models that make up the health care delivery system and the differences in the environments in which those organizations operate. To be successful, we must provide a variety of payment approaches that apply to different organizational structures, while creating requirements and rewards to help provider organizations evolve to meet the needs of their communities. This can be done by clarifying the outcomes we expect from the health system and aligning payments to reward the achievement of those outcomes, while remaining flexible about how they are to be achieved.

The right incentives can encourage providers to work together, in formal organizations or in looser relationships, to take broader responsibility for the patients they treat and the resources they use—and to allow them to benefit from doing so. As organizational arrangements evolve, payment methods can be adjusted to encourage and reward increasing levels of accountability, with continuous development and improvement over time. But even over time, different payment approaches and organizational models may be required in different areas and different circumstances to accomplish the goals of health reform.

This mix of reforms to how we pay, how our health system is organized, and how it delivers care is essential to address our burgeoning health care costs and improve the quality of that care over time. To accomplish this, we would repeal the SGR mechanism that has impeded attempts to rationalize Medicare payment; adjust payment rates to reflect the value of care and its contribution to better health and outcomes; develop, implement, and support alternative payment arrangements; and encourage movement away from unfettered fee-for-service. Immediate action is required, but that action must address both short-term needs and long-term goals, to produce better health, better care, and lower costs so access to affordable care is a reality for generations to come.

Medicare Should Stop Using Profit-Driven Fee-for-Service Providers

Phillip Longman

Phillip Longman is a senior fellow at Washington Monthly, *a bimonthly nonprofit magazine focused on US politics and government, and the New America Foundation, a nonprofit public policy institute and think tank located in Washington, DC.*

While the partisan gap in Washington is wider than it's been at any time in living memory, the two parties do have one remarkable agenda in common. Both have proposed cuts in Medicare so drastic that they would have been politically suicidal a decade ago and may still be. Yet neither party is backing off.

Declaring War on Medicare

All but six Republicans in the House of Representatives have voted to turn Medicare into a voucher program—a vision endorsed by all the GOP's [Republican Party's] major presidential candidates as well. Under the proposal, famously crafted by Representative Paul Ryan, each senior citizen would receive only a fixed amount of money (about $8,000 on average in 2022) to spend on private health care insurance each year, regardless of what his or her health care needs and costs might actually be. The Congressional Budget Office (CBO) estimates that under the plan, seniors would pay about 68 percent of their health care costs out of their own pockets in 2030, as compared to 25 percent to 30 percent under traditional Medicare.

Democrats rightly characterize this plan as "ending Medicare as we know it," but both President [Barack] Obama and party leaders agree that deep cuts in Medicare spending must happen soon. "With an aging population and rising health care costs, we are spending too fast to sustain the program," the president told a joint session of Congress on September 8 [2011]. As part of his most recent deficit reduction plan, he has proposed $248 billion in Medicare savings over the next ten years. This includes higher copays for many beneficiaries and steep cuts in payments to providers. If you think Obama and the Democrats are bluffing, consider that the health care law they passed last year came with hundreds of millions in Medicare cuts and includes a mechanism that could cut vastly more. And though the president in September came out against Republican plans to raise the Medicare retirement age to sixty-seven, in the debt limit negotiations earlier this year he signaled his willingness to go along with it.

> *The GOP's privatization plan won't actually cut health care costs, but ... the Democrats' ideas ... are unlikely to bend the cost curve anywhere near far enough.*

Then there's the new Joint Select Committee on Deficit Reduction—aka the "super committee"—on which the president has also put his signature. By the end of the year, Congress must take an up-or-down vote on the recommendations of a majority of the committee, which are likely to include steep cuts to Medicare and, possibly, increases in the retirement age and other restrictions on eligibility. In the event the committee deadlocks, across-the-board spending cuts, including some to Medicare, go into effect.

Why are both parties declaring war on Medicare when both know that it could lead to their own political annihilation? The reason is simple. While both Democrats and Republicans fear the wrath of the AARP [American Association of

Retired Persons, an advocacy group for older Americans] and the exploding ranks of hard-pressed seniors—to say nothing of lobbies like the American Hospital Association—Medicare's relentless squeeze on the budget seems to party leaders to give them no choice but to attack the program's spending regardless of the political cost. Medicare's ever-expanding claims on the treasury threaten to crowd out nearly every other priority on either party's agenda, from bullet trains and decent public schools to, yes, avoiding future tax increases and draconian cuts in the military.

The federal government should do the following: announce a day certain and near when Medicare will be out of the business of subsidizing profit-driven, fee-for-service medicine.

The U.S. wouldn't even face a structural deficit, much less have to endure the downgrading of its credit rating, were it not for the cost of Medicare (and, to a lesser extent, Medicaid). Just the projected increase in the cost of these two programs over the next twenty years is equivalent to doubling the Pentagon's current budget, and there is no end in sight after that. By contrast, Social Security will rise only gradually, from 4.8 percent of GDP [gross domestic product, a measure of the country's total economic output] to 6.1 percent in 2035, and then taper off as the large Baby Boom generation passes. Meanwhile, according to the same CBO projection, all other government programs—the military, the courts, farm subsidies, Amtrak, infrastructure spending, education, and so on— are on course to shrink dramatically as a share of the economy, from 12.3 percent of GDP in 2011 to 8.5 percent in 2035. As others have observed, the federal government is not so gradually being transformed into a giant, and insolvent, health insurance company.

We can at least be thankful that both parties are sane enough to recognize the problem and brave enough to offer politically courageous proposals to solve it. But here's the bad news: neither side's solution is likely to work. The GOP's privatization plan won't actually cut health care costs, but merely shifts them to individuals. Meanwhile, the Democrats' ideas, though offering more in the way of actual reform, are unlikely to bend the cost curve anywhere near far enough. Moreover, by focusing so much on cutting reimbursement rates to doctors without directly attacking the colossal inefficiency of the U.S. health care system, the Democrats' approach runs the very real risk that it will lead to a severe shortage of doctors willing to treat Medicare patients.

A Better Idea

Here's a better idea—one that offers a relatively painless and proven fix that will also vastly improve the quality of U.S. health care. Approximately a third of all Medicare spending goes for unnecessary surgeries, redundant testing, and other forms of overtreatment, according to well-accepted estimates. The largest single reason for this extraordinary volume of wasteful and often dangerous overtreatment is Medicare's use of the "fee-for-service" method of compensating health care providers that dominates U.S. medicine, under which doctors and hospitals are rewarded according to how many procedures and tests they perform. To fix this, the federal government should do the following: *announce a day certain and near when Medicare will be out of the business of subsidizing profit-driven, fee-for-service medicine.*

Going forward, Medicare should instead contract exclusively with health care providers like the Mayo Clinic, Kaiser Permanente, the Cleveland Clinic, Intermountain Health Care, the Geisinger Health System, or even the Veterans Health Administration [VA]. All these are nonprofit, mission-driven, managed care organizations widely heralded by health care experts for their combination of cost-effectiveness and high quality, including cutting-edge use of electronic medical records, adherence to protocols of care based on science, and avoidance of medical errors. Because doctors working at these institutions are not compensated on a fee-for-service basis, they are neither rewarded for performing unnecessary tests and surgeries nor penalized financially for keeping their patients well. And unlike for-profit HMOs [health maintenance organizations], these institutions are not pressured by shareholders to maximize earnings through withholding appropriate care.

By the late 1990s, the spread of health maintenance organizations and other forms of managed care virtually eliminated health care inflation in the United States, providing a brief moment—not seen since—when the cost of health care did not outpace average wage increases. That triumph in cost containment had its downsides, to be sure, namely the corrupting entry of profit-driven institutions that undermined medical professionalism and often led to denial of needed care. But with the benefit of hindsight, we can avoid repeating those mistakes and reinvigorate the once idealistic and highly effective managed care movement by insisting that Medicare providers also be nonprofit institutions. If we have to control the cost of Medicare, why not do it this way?...

The Trouble with Previous HMO Reforms

For ten years during the 1980s and '90s, Americans embraced and then rejected HMOs and managed care. While the experiment in widespread managed care ultimately failed to reshape American health care, much can be learned by examining what worked and what didn't.

Today, many Americans view HMOs simply as organizations designed to make money by denying them care. And it's a sad fact that many HMOs have wound up doing just that, or else using clever marketing techniques to make sure they cherry-pick only young and healthy customers who are un-likely to get sick. But it is important to remember that HMOs and other forms of managed care came into existence in large measure because of a big problem that is still with us and get-ting worse—namely, vast amounts of poorly coordinated, ex-cessive, and dangerous treatment.

Care providers would be prepaid a set amount per patient . . . [to] give 'doctors an incentive to keep people healthy.'

The original vision of those who championed HMOs was that this new model of care would vastly improve the quality of American medicine and only incidentally lower its cost. Paul Ellwood, a pediatrician who more than any other single advocate built the case for HMOs starting in the late 1960s, put it this way: "My own most compelling interest as a physi-cian was in the integration of health care, quality accountabil-ity, and consumer choices based on quality first and, second-arily, price."

What Ellwood and other reformers wanted more specifi-cally was an "integrated delivery system" in which primary care physicians would coordinate care in large, multispecialty medical group practices that would in turn be part of a coor-dinated system of hospitals, labs, and pharmacies. Moreover, to address the problems of overtreatment and lack of preven-tion, care providers would be prepaid a set amount per pa-tient. As Alain Enthoven, another champion of managed care, once wrote, this would give "doctors an incentive to keep people healthy."

Such were the highly idealistic and data-driven concerns and issues behind the emergence of HMOs. What went wrong? Eventually, HMOs morphed into many different forms and hybrids. Some were nonprofits, others were publicly traded companies answerable to Wall Street. Some were "staff models" that put physicians on salary and effectively eliminated the problem of intentional overtreatment; others became little more than loose networks of doctors on contract. Some were run by idealists, others by shysters, crooks, and knaves who convinced themselves that the road to riches could be found by low-balling on prepaid contracts and then denying their patients necessary care.

Even the many HMOs that tried to do the right thing often ran into a fundamental flaw in their business model. Most remained small enough that the majority of their customers changed plans every few years, either because they moved to a different market or because their employers switched to a cheaper plan. For all but the largest HMOs, this circumstance demolished the business case for prevention and effective management of long-term conditions like diabetes. Before any returns from investing in a patient's long-term health could be realized, the patient was likely to be enrolled in some other plan. According to Lawrence P. Casalino, a professor of public health at Weill Cornell Medical College who has extensively interviewed HMO executives, the common view in the industry is "Why should I spend our money to save money for our competitors?"

By the 1990s, most people who were enrolled in any particular HMO had little or no choice in the matter; they were there because their employers were trying to save money. It didn't help that many fee-for-service doctors felt threatened by the growing dominance of HMOs and other managed care providers and complained to their patients about it. Neither was the industry's image helped by the negative press and lawsuits that some HMOs attracted.

High-Performing Managed Care Organizations

The result was a public backlash. But with the benefit of hindsight, we can see that it didn't have to turn out this way. We only have to look at the big exceptions to the often poor performance of managed care organizations over the last several decades. These are institutions with high levels of patient satisfaction that are also lauded by health care quality researchers for their patient safety, adherence to evidence-based protocols of care, and general cost-effectiveness. They include integrated providers like Intermountain Health Care, the Cleveland Clinic, the Mayo Clinic, Geisinger Health System, Kaiser Permanente, and the VA, the last of which ranks highest of all on most cost and quality metrics and is in effect the largest, and purest, nonprofit, staff-model HMO in the land (though, of course, government run and open only to veterans). The VA's cost per patient is about 21 percent below what it would cost under Medicare to serve the same population with the same level of benefits. Until the wars in Iraq and Afghanistan heated up, the VA was also holding increases in its cost per patient down to just 1.7 percent a year, compared to annual increases of nearly 30 percent for Medicare.

Medicare beneficiaries [should] . . . have the choice of deciding among competing managed care organizations that meet specific quality requirements.

What do these exceptions to the rule have in common? First, they are all large enough to achieve significant economies of scale. The VA's scale, for example, has also been an important precondition for the deployment of its highly effective system of electronic medical records, the cost of which it has been able to spread across a large base of hospitals and clinics. So too with Kaiser Permanente and the other examples of "best-practice" health care delivery systems mentioned above. The size of these institutions also means that the data generated by their digitalized information technology about what works and what doesn't has far greater scientific value because the records are drawn from a very broad population.

And their scale allows them to integrate and coordinate care among a broad range of specialists who all work for the same institution and use the same patient records so that the care patients receive is far less fragmented (and dangerous) than found generally in fee-for-service medicine.

Furthermore, large size gives these institutions substantial market power to negotiate favorable deals with drug companies and other medical suppliers. The VA enjoys a 48 percent discount in the price it pays for frequently prescribed drugs compared to those obtained by even the next-biggest health care plans. The size of the VA also allows it to push past the cartels, known as group purchasing organizations, that control the prices paid by smaller health care providers for hospital supplies, from hypodermics to bed linens.

Providers qualified for reimbursement under Medicare would have to be nonprofit organizations [and] . . . use salaried doctors.

Finally, and just as importantly, the size of these institutions allows them to hold on to a significant portion of their customers year after year. This, along with their nonprofit status, preserves a business case for prevention and investment in long-term health. Unlike for-profit HMOs, they are not under pressure to maximize short-term profits by withholding appropriate care; instead, all their incentives are aligned toward providing enough care, and no more than is necessary, to keep their patients healthy over the long term.

Medicare Managed Care Reforms

We should set a date when the Medicare system will stop covering fee-for-service medicine. Medicare beneficiaries would instead have the choice of deciding among competing managed care organizations that meet specific quality requirements. These organizations wouldn't be standard for-profit

HMOs. And they would not receive the inflated, no-questions-asked reimbursement rates that have prevailed under the Medicare Advantage program. Nor would they be anything as amorphous and underdefined as an accountable care organization.

Instead, providers qualified for reimbursement under Medicare would have to be nonprofit organizations to start with. They'd also have to use salaried doctors, deploy integrated health information like the VA and other best-in-class health care providers do, adhere to evidence-based protocols of care, and operate under a fixed budget. Specifically, for every Medicare patient who decided to join their plan, the government would pay a specific annual reimbursement based on that patient's age. These Medicare-certified providers would not be allowed to turn away patients on Medicare or kick such patients out of their plans. In order to stay in the program, they would have to meet strict safety and quality requirements on such measures as hospital-acquired infection rates. And they would have to be at least of a certain size to participate.

The latter requirement would allow them to achieve the economies and other benefits of scale described above. With enough large institutions participating, the government could assure that no single one monopolized a local market and that seniors always had a choice of plans.

The best of our integrated health care providers would instantly qualify. With that advantage, top-flight regional providers like Mayo, Intermountain, and the Cleveland Clinic would have an incentive to expand geographically. The VA, which is already national in scope, could be allowed to expand by serving the many older veterans who are currently excluded from the system because they lack service-related disabilities or are not poor enough to meet the VA's means test.

By allowing these older vets to use their Medicare entitlement for VA care, and perhaps their elderly spouses as well, everyone would win.

Meanwhile, many existing health care providers that didn't qualify would face a choice: they could merge with institutions that already deliver the high quality health care necessary to become a Medicare-certified provider and adapt to their cultures and protocols care, or they could reform themselves. Under the threat of losing their ability to collect from Medicare, they would find it much easier to stare down greedy, profit-driven specialists and others resistant to change and gain the power they needed as an institution to do the right thing.

If you reform the delivery of Medicare, you just might reform the entire health care system.

Raising any capital needed to reform an existing institution, or to create a new one eligible to treat Medicare patients, should not be a serious obstacle. Banks and investment firms would gladly extend credit and capital to any institution that could show a reasonable plan for meeting the requirements, because such institutions would have a predictable future revenue stream that could be used as collateral. Our financial system routinely does this for other nonprofit entities that have predictable revenue streams, from cities and counties to universities, as well as certain hospitals with assured earnings.

Indeed, institutions that became certified to serve the Medicare population under this proposal could reasonably hope to attract many younger Americans, especially those who will become mandated by the ACA [Affordable Care Act] to purchase health coverage starting in 2014. Benefiting from an inherently efficient model of care, these institutions will be the thrifty option for fulfilling the individual mandate, while also happening to be the smart option as well. They may also be attractive to middle-age Americans contemplating retirement, who may want to transition early into the system that will wind up treating them into old age. Indeed, the government may even want to encourage this kind of behavior, given that the longer an HMO is on the hook for a patient's care, the more financial incentive it has to keep the patient healthy. These and other effects could ripple through the system, hinting at a bigger truth: if you reform the delivery of Medicare, you just might reform the entire health care system.

The Advantage of Managed Care Reforms

Would there be resistance to such a proposal? Of course. But compared to what?

Let's start from the point of view of individual citizens. Yes, many current Medicare beneficiaries would be upset by any change to the status quo. But these folks could and probably should be allowed to stay in traditional Medicare; the changes outlined here will take some years to put in place in any event. The people who will be affected first are those eligible for Medicare in, say, ten years.

Most of us who are now approaching retirement age or are younger have spent our entire lives living with, and largely accepting, some constraints on our choice of doctor, if only through the limits imposed by preferred provider networks. Personally, not once since I was still young in the early 1980s have I been part of a health insurance plan that allowed me to choose any doctor I wanted without paying a financial penalty, and I've had what by the standards of the times has been "gold-plated" coverage. Almost the only people left in America who don't face such restraints are current beneficiaries of fee-for-service Medicare.

That said, a plan like this could still provide future Medicare beneficiaries with plenty of options. In addition to being able to choose among competing Medicare-eligible HMOs, seniors should also be free to use their own money to pay to see any doctor they want or to access experimental drugs or un-proven treatments that the HMOs (wisely) won't cover. If the "price" of preserving Medicare is that some of us will be sometimes forced to go "out of network" and pay more of our own money to receive some kinds of care, then I think younger Americans already inured to the practice will almost certainly be willing to pay it.

To those who disagree, we could offer an additional choice: If you wait until you are, say, age seventy to apply for Medi-care, then the system will cover you for the same wasteful fee-for-service medicine your parents currently get. But if you want to be covered at age sixty-five, you'll have to agree to re-ceive your care from a Medicare-certified nonprofit HMO.

These are tough choices, no doubt. But ask yourself: Do they sound all that onerous when compared to the competing policy proposals already on the table, such as turning Medi-care into a voucher program that leaves all of us responsible in old age for paying 70 percent of our own health care costs, or seeing Medicare reimbursement rates reduced to the point that we can't find a doctor who will treat us, or having to wait until age sixty-seven before being eligible for Medicare at all?

We can certainly expect lots of opposition from well-heeled practitioners of for-profit medicine—all those cardiologists making a killing doing unnecessary stent operations, for ex-ample. And we'll hear from many prestigious academic medi-cal centers, an unfortunate number of which engage in mas-sive amounts of overtreatment because they are dominated by specialists who look down their nose at doctors engaged in "mere" primary care.

Yet as difficult as these challenges will be, reformers are now armed with abundant, peer-reviewed proof of just how dangerous and wasteful fee-for-service medicine has become, and the public has begun to catch on as well. Ten years ago, for example, researchers were just beginning to document how the death toll of medical errors, hospital infections, and inappropriate treatment had conspired to make contact with the health care system the third leading cause of death in the United States. Today, these facts are widely accepted by health care experts and generally understood by policy makers at the highest levels of government. Educated Americans have read about them in the newspapers, and most citizens who have spent any time in a typical hospital trying to make sure a loved one gets her proper medicine on time have experienced firsthand the extent of routine system breakdown.

Some conservatives, no doubt, will instinctively align themselves with the forces of for-profit, fee-for-service medicine, or be lured into doing so by heaps of campaign contributions. Many Democrats as well can be counted on to carry water for prestigious but deeply wasteful and dangerous academic medical centers, which tend to be concentrated in Deep Blue [Democratic] zones like New York, Boston, and Los Angeles. So yes, enacting this proposal will not be easy.

Americans can have their cake and eat it too. We can improve our health care while lowering its cost, and in the process eliminate our long-term deficits and resume building for the future.

But then, ask yourself again, compared to what? Both parties have already signed on to changes to Medicare that are hardly less radical, will be resisted by powerful interest groups, and risk the wrath of voters. Moreover, these proposals are not really solutions, because they either shift the inflating cost of health care onto individual Americans or cut reimbursement rates to a point where Medicare is "saved" on paper but in the real world has little value to elders who can't find a doctor. By contrast, this approach directly attacks the root problem, which is the waste and inefficiency caused by fee-for-service medicine.

And as politically difficult as the road to this solution may be, it does give each side things it wants. It allows Democrats to say that they will not cut benefits to Medicare recipients. And Democrats should also like that these nongovernmental organizations serving the Medicare population will have the freedom to do things liberals have long wanted Medicare itself to do, like bargain with drug companies for lower prices. Meanwhile, Republicans who support this proposal will be able to boast that it takes vast decision-making power out of the hands of "unelected bureaucrats in the federal government" and puts that power in the hands of private organizations that compete with each other for customers. Under this approach, Medicare officials won't have to figure out how to write regulations on what specific drugs and procedures are not appropriate medicine; they'll be contracting out those details to private-sector organizations and simply holding them accountable for results, such as keeping a high percentage of their patients healthy and managing their conditions effectively.

Let's close by stressing the positive. America is still a rich and productive country. Compared to Europe or Japan, it has a youthful population and no real long-term debt crisis except that caused by huge volumes of wasteful and dangerous fee-for-service medicine. So once again in our long history, Americans can have their cake and eat it too. We can improve our health care while lowering its cost, and in the process eliminate our long-term deficits and resume building for the future.

So why don't we feel more optimistic? Because there is this feeling of despair, especially among policy makers and the chattering classes, that we don't know how, politically, to bring health care costs in line. We know that all other developed countries get better health care for less money, and that it is no real mystery how they do it. But all their approaches seem—or can be spun as—socialistic, paternalistic, and fundamentally un-American, and therefore impossible to consider.

Yet we have within our reach a solution that is not imported from abroad, and that has been proved on our own shores by all-American institutions, from our best nonprofit HMOs to the VA health system. We may not currently have the political will to use these institutions as the model and means to fix the health care crisis, and hence eliminate our long-term fiscal problems. But we shouldn't fool ourselves into thinking it can't be done.

Market-Based Reform Is Necessary for Medicare

James C. Capretta

James C. Capretta is a fellow at the Ethics and Public Policy Center (EPPC), a conservative public policy organization that advocates for limited government. He also was an associate director at the White House Office of Management and Budget (OMB) from 2001 to 2004, where he had responsibility for health care, Social Security, education, and welfare programs.

Rapidly rising health care costs threaten to push the federal budget past the breaking point. In 1975, total federal spending on Medicare and Medicaid was 1.3 percent of gross domestic product (GDP) [a measure of the country's total economic output]. In 2010, it was 5.5 percent. The Congressional Budget Office (CBO) expects spending on these programs, together with spending on the entitlement expansions in the 2010 health law, to reach 9.7 percent of GDP by 2030.

At the heart of the budget and entitlement problem is Medicare, the health insurance program for those who are age 65 and older as well as millions of disabled Americans. With spending of $525 billion in 2010, Medicare is the largest payer for medical services in the United States. Its size and market dominance heavily influence how all of American health care is organized.

Analysts who have offered proposals to slow the pace of rising Medicare costs tend to fall into one of two competing camps. The first camp believes that central government management of prices and government reengineering of how services are delivered by doctors and hospitals can control Medicare's costs—as well as costs in the wider health system—without harming the quality of care. The other camp argues that strong competition in a functioning marketplace will work far better than more government micromanagement to improve quality and reduce costs.

Over the past three decades, the camp that favors government control and regulation has been calling the shots in the Medicare program, without success.

Government Control Versus Market Forces

The gulf between these two camps is deep. They represent completely different approaches to resource allocation—one centered on government control and the political process and the other on consumer choice. The divide is so deep that it is widely viewed on both sides as unbridgeable. As a result, every health care debate tends to become deeply polarized.

Over the past three decades, the camp that favors government control and regulation has been calling the shots in the Medicare program, without success. Medicare spending has continued to rise very rapidly, and the program is now projected to become insolvent in 2024 due to mounting costs.

The alternative to top-down cost control is the financial discipline of a functioning marketplace, which holds costs in check in other sectors of the American economy—something that most Americans understand from buying groceries, electronics, and services.

Recently, proposals have been advanced that would bring market discipline to Medicare by converting the program into fixed premium assistance instead of an open-ended, defined-benefit entitlement. These reforms are designed to harness the power of competition to increase efficiency in the Medicare program.

These reform plans have met with fierce criticism in some quarters. A primary argument of opponents is that government-led efforts will work better than competition to control costs without compromising the quality of care for patients. However, a careful review of the history of Medicare and other programs shows that this criticism is wrong. Competition can bring more discipline to the program, whereas the alternative—top-down price controls—will seriously erode the quality of care that seniors and other patients receive.

Medicare, as currently constituted, is a primary cause of the cost problem for all of American health care.

Medicare's Relationship to the Broader Health System

Most often, those who believe that more forceful central management of the health system is the solution to rising costs have viewed Medicare as something like a railcar hooked onto a runaway freight train; The only way to slow down Medicare would be to slow down the whole train. Thus, their solutions tend to aim at containing costs systemwide with more government control, such as a global budget or an all-payer rate-setting system in which public and private insurers alike pay the same government-set prices for services.

Of course, those who believe in building a marketplace for health care reject these kinds of reforms. Their solutions would move Medicare and the rest of the health system toward more cost-conscious consumption.

Interestingly, in the debate over the recently enacted health law, a subtle shift occurred in the thinking among some of those who favor more government control. Instead of viewing Medicare as an innocent bystander in the cost-escalation problem, these analysts began to see that Medicare, as currently constituted, is a primary cause of the cost problem for all of American health care.

Most of those who hold this view, especially those who supported passage of the Patient Protection and Affordable Care Act (PPACA), have not acknowledged and probably will not acknowledge this shift in their point of view, but they do not need to acknowledge it, because it is obvious in the remedies that they pushed in the health care law. PPACA proponents argued repeatedly throughout the legislative process that "delivery system reform" would be the only way to slow cost growth and build a more efficient health sector. In other words, they supported reforms that would alter the ways in which physicians and hospitals provide services to patients. To bring about this "reform of the delivery system," they argued that Medicare must change how it pays for services for its enrollees.

This is an important development. It does not bridge the huge divide between the governmentalists and those who support market-based reforms, but it does reveal a growing understanding that Medicare's current design not only is *not* the solution to America's health care problems, but actually is the source of many of those problems. Other factors also drive up costs, including unreformed medical malpractice laws, open-ended federal tax subsidization of job-based insurance, perverse incentives in the federal–state matching program for Medicaid, lack of price transparency, and the growing demand for better medical care that comes with increasing wealth and higher incomes. However, Medicare is the most important reason that health care is expensive and needlessly inefficient in the United States.

Outdated Model

American health care has its virtues. The system of job-based insurance for working-age people and Medicare for retirees provides ready access to care for most citizens, although the poor have more problems accessing care through Medicaid. Americans have highly skilled physicians and capital-intensive inpatient institutions that can deliver medical miracles for the sickest. U.S. health care is also open to medical innovation in ways that other health systems around the world are not.

Yet health care in the U.S. is often highly inefficient, and the system is extremely fragmented. Physicians, hospitals, clinics, labs, and pharmacies are autonomous, financially independent units. They bill separately when they render services, with very little coordination of care, which leads to a disastrous level of duplicative services and low-quality care that is dangerous for the patient. The bureaucracy is maddening, the paperwork is burdensome and excessive, and providers have little regard for making the care experience convenient and pleasant.

Indeed, the pervasiveness of these problems has led numerous analysts and scholars to recommend that U.S. health care move toward a true consumer marketplace. Mark Pauly of the University of Pennsylvania and Joseph Antos of the American Enterprise Institute have proposed using marketplace incentives to create a system that is more responsive to patients even as it achieves communitywide objectives, such as better coverage for low-income households and those with chronic health conditions.

Patients must pay some of the cost when they receive health care services. Otherwise, there is no financial check against the understandable inclination to agree to all of the tests, consultations, and procedures that could be possible.

The Medicare Fee-for-Service Failure

At the heart of all of this dysfunction is Medicare—more precisely, Medicare's dominant fee-for-service (FFS) insurance structure. . . .

Medicare's FFS insurance is the largest and most influential payer in most markets. As the name implies, FFS pays any licensed health care provider when a Medicare patient uses services—no questions asked. More than 75 percent of Medicare's 35 million enrollees are in the FFS program. Physicians, hospitals, clinics, and other care organizations most often set up their operations to maximize revenue from Medicare FFS payments.

For FFS insurance to make any economic sense at all, patients must pay some of the cost when they receive health care services. Otherwise, there is no financial check against the understandable inclination to agree to all of the tests, consultations, and procedures that could be possible, but not guaranteed, steps to better health.

However, Medicare's FFS does not have effective cost-sharing at the point of service. The program requires cost-sharing, including 20 percent coinsurance to see a physician, but more than 90 percent of FFS beneficiaries have additional insurance in the form of Medigap coverage, retiree wrap-around plans, or Medicaid that pays for nearly all costs not covered by FFS. Further, Medicare's rules require providers to accept the Medicare reimbursement rates as payment in full, effectively precluding any additional billing to the patient.

In the vast majority of cases, FFS enrollees incur no additional cost when they use more services, and health care providers earn more only when service use rises. Given these parameters, it is not surprising that the volume of services used by FFS participants has exploded over the years. To make matters worse, the taxpayers pay 80 percent of the increased cost induced by Medigap coverage. Medigap premiums cover only the 20 percent (coinsurance and deductibles) that Medicare does not pay. This serious price distortion leads to overconsumption of Medigap coverage. . . .

Medicare administrators have understood the problems created by Medicare's FFS payment systems for many years.

Despite the rising volume, they have tried to control costs by increasing scrutiny of the payment rates per service. Indeed, the ongoing maintenance of the arcane and complex payment systems for hospitals, physicians, nursing homes, and other provider categories is an all-consuming enterprise for the Medicare bureaucracy and the provider groups that watch the bureaucracy's every move.

Despite curbing some abuses, these payment systems have not controlled Medicare costs. As often happens, the regulated have learned how to work the regulator. Politicians and program officials do not want to be accused of disrupting how and where seniors get care, so care providers naturally use exactly that threat—closed facilities and reduced service—to narrow the range of possible payment changes from year to year. The yearly ritual of keeping physician fees at least level with the prior year's fees is just one example of this phenomenon. With an effective "political" floor on their Medicare payments, many health care providers see no reason to move away from their autonomous structures and integrate with others in a more organized system of care.

The Centrally Planned "Solution"

Although there is growing recognition of the problems in Medicare's current design, the opposing sides are proposing very different solutions.

Proponents of the 2010 health care law observed the problem and concluded that better technocratic solutions were needed. They argue incorrectly that today's arrangements—with all of the distortions that come from open-ended taxpayer subsidization of third-party insurance—are the result of a "private" market that has not worked. They then conclude that, because the market has failed and cannot fix the prevalent problems in health care, the solution is more intensive government regulation. From their perspective, the antidote to today's inefficient delivery arrangements is a top-down payment reform program in which the federal government uses the leverage of Medicare payment policy to build essentially new organizational arrangements for providing care to patients. . . .

Premium Support Can Transform Health-Care Delivery

The alternative to the failed top-down approach of government micromanagement is to create the supportive environment for a properly functioning marketplace in Medicare. Medicare does not operate that way today, which is why the program needs reform. The most important feature of such a marketplace system is cost-conscious consumers choosing among competing insurers and delivery systems based on price and quality. That is the basis for The Heritage Foundation's Medicare proposal in *Saving the American Dream* and the proposal that was included in the House budget resolution for fiscal year 2012.

Instead of a defined-benefit entitlement, new Medicare beneficiaries would decide how to use a fixed-dollar contribution provided by Medicare.

Of course, both the Heritage plan and the House-passed budget are much more than plans for Medicare reform. They are comprehensive plans to put the nation's finances on a sustainable trajectory with policies that will promote economic growth and prosperity.

Yet both plans hinge on converting Medicare into a premium-support program for new entrants below a certain age. Instead of a defined-benefit entitlement, new Medicare beneficiaries would decide how to use a fixed-dollar contribution provided by Medicare. In general, the beneficiaries would decide which insurance plans they preferred. If the premiums for their plans were higher than the Medicare contribution, they would pay the difference out of their own resources. If they chose less expensive plans, they would pay lower premiums and keep the savings. This structure would provide a powerful incentive for the program's participants to find high-value plans that charge low premiums.

Critics argue that this type of reform would not control health care costs, but would only shift the burden and risk of rapidly rising costs onto individuals because the government's financial support for Medicare would no longer keep pace with premium growth. However, this is the wrong way to look at these reforms because it ignores the evidence that functioning markets, not top-down regulation and planning, are the key to obtaining value for money and restraining spending. The goal is not to shift rising premium costs from the government onto the beneficiaries, but to move away from the cost-increasing incentives of Medicare FFS and create an entirely different market dynamic to achieve greater efficiency and cost-effectiveness. In time, implementation of a premium-support model would convert millions of passive Medicare participants into cost-conscious consumers of insurance and alternative models for securing needed medical services.

With cost-conscious consumers looking for the best value for their money, cost-cutting innovations would be rewarded, not punished as they are today. Physicians and hospitals would have strong financial incentives to reorganize themselves to increase productivity and efficiency in order to capture a larger share of what would become a highly competitive marketplace. This is the way to slow the growth of health care costs. Indeed, it is the only way to slow growing costs without harming the quality of care.

Prominent health analysts have been making the case that competition in health care could produce much higher value and lower costs than are produced by heavy-handed government payment regulation. Alain Enthoven, one of the original architects of the managed competition theory of health care reform, has written numerous articles on the benefits of competition in various health care markets, including the California public employees system. He and Mark Pauly of the University of Pennsylvania have been among the most prominent and respected economists who have championed vigorous price competition in Medicare as the solution to the cost problem.

Their view that competition can bring more discipline to Medicare spending is supported by experience with the Medicare prescription drug benefit and the Federal Employees Health Benefits Program (FEHBP). It is also supported by official cost estimates of the effects of premium support. Most important, the Chief Actuary of the Medicare program, the official most responsible for assessing Medicare's future financial viability, shares this view. . . .

Transforming American Medical Care

No one, not even the CBO, knows for certain how much a reformed Medicare program based on consumer choice and competition would slow the pace of rising health care costs. The relevant data needed to estimate the effects of such a substantial change in incentives are difficult to find. At the end of the day, policymakers will need to judge the likelihood that such a reform would succeed. Policymakers need to decide which policy approach is most likely to lead to a virtuous cycle of productivity improvement and higher quality throughout the health sector. Given the track record, it is not reasonable to expect top-down reforms, such as those in the new health care law, to produce the desired improvements.

However, a well-functioning marketplace would set in motion the forces needed to transform American medical care, including in the Medicare context, into a model of efficient patient-centered care. Policymakers have good reason to conclude that American health care would benefit from the transformational power of the marketplace that has consistently improved products and services in other sectors of the U.S. and global economies.

The government can and should play an important oversight role in such a reformed system, but the difficult organizational changes and innovations needed to provide better care at lower cost must come from the bottom up, not from the top down. In other words, changes should come from those who are delivering services to patients, not from Congress, the Department of Health and Human Services, or an appointed board of remote and unaccountable "experts."

Sharing Costs Is No Way to Fix Medicare

Peter R. Orszag

Peter R. Orszag is an adjunct senior fellow at the Council on Foreign Relations, an independent think tank and publisher, as well as vice chairman of global banking at Citigroup, an international financial conglomerate. He also served as director of the Office of Management and Budget (OMB) under President Barack Obama.

Many Republican policy makers appear conflicted about the budget plan put forward by the House Budget Committee chairman, Representative Paul Ryan of Wisconsin. They are torn because they like its substance, but believe it is bad politics, especially among elderly voters. In truth, the substance is not particularly appealing either.

At the heart of the Ryan plan is a shift within Medicare toward consumer-directed health care—which in turn is predicated on increasing beneficiaries' "skin in the game" to make the health system more efficient.

While more consumer cost-sharing would help reduce unnecessary care, the plan would not live up to its billing in cutting health costs for America. According to the nonpartisan Congressional Budget Office, it would do the opposite. That's right: The CBO found that the Ryan Medicare proposal would substantially increase total health-care spending.

Before delving into the Ryan plan in more detail, let's take a quick detour into why consumer-directed health-care reform—though useful to some degree—may not be the panacea it's often held out to be. The core problem is that health-care costs are concentrated among expensive treatments for chronic diseases and end-of-life care—and even consumer-directed approaches retain deep third-party insurance against such cases (which is, after all, the whole point of insurance). Consider that, if you rank Medicare beneficiaries by cost, one-quarter of patients account for more than 85 percent of total costs. So even if the other 75 percent spend less on doctors and medicine, they can't take a significant bite out of the total.

Experiments with Cost-Sharing

Perhaps the most famous research on consumer cost-sharing is the RAND Health Insurance Experiment, which was conducted with 2,750 families from 1971 to 1982. Each family was randomly assigned to one of five formulas determining how much of their medical expenses they would pay themselves.

It is no great accomplishment, however, merely to shift health expenditures from the federal government to consumers, without doing anything to decrease them in total.

The RAND results showed that the introduction of cost-sharing can reduce medical spending without causing harm to health—that holy grail of health policy. The biggest reductions in the RAND study, though, came in moving from zero expense for families to at least some cost-sharing. As we already have some cost-sharing in our current system (co-pays and deductibles), that finding doesn't suggest a new path to savings. And, unfortunately, the results from raising cost-sharing above current levels were generally more modest.

Cutting Back on Medicine

Other evidence, from studies of employers that have adopted consumer-directed approaches in the form of high-deductible health plans such as health savings accounts, is similarly mixed. Significant cost reductions typically occur in the first year, perhaps because of pent-up demand for health services, but these are often partially if not fully reversed in the second and third years. And some of this research has highlighted a longer-term concern: To save money in the short run, people tend to cut back on crucial medicines. This could lead to higher medical costs over time.

Which brings us back to the Ryan plan. Under that proposal, starting in 2022, the government would issue new Medicare beneficiaries a payment that they could use to purchase private insurance. These payments would increase in line with the consumer price index but not with faster-rising health costs. The slower increase in payments would generate large savings (and less risk) for the federal government; indeed, this would be the single most important driver of savings from the Ryan budget plan as a whole.

Beneficiaries Pay More

As the government paid relatively less for Medicare, beneficiaries would bear an increasing share of the cost of their care. It is no great accomplishment, however, merely to shift health expenditures from the federal government to consumers, without doing anything to decrease them in total.

The CBO's analysis of the Ryan plan confirms that federal expenditures would be reduced, by a lot. By 2030, payments for a typical beneficiary would be more than 20 percent lower than current projections, according to the report, and the beneficiary's personal costs would increase.

So far, nothing unexpected. On the critical metric of whether the Ryan plan would reduce total health-care costs, though, the CBO conclusion is shocking: The plan would not only fail to decrease health-care costs per beneficiary, it would increase them—by an astonishingly large amount that grows over time. By 2030, health spending on the typical beneficiary would be more than 40 percent higher under the Ryan plan than under existing Medicare, according to the CBO report. Health-care costs would not be reduced on the backs of seniors; they would be raised on the backs of seniors.

Cost-Containment Machine

How could this possibly be, when the point of reform is to reduce costs? The CBO points to two factors: Private plans have higher administrative costs than the federal Medicare program, and less negotiating leverage with providers.

Everything in life is relative. The CBO's analysis of the health-reform act that was passed last year was, well, lukewarm on its potential to reduce costs. Compared with the Ryan plan, though, the health reform act comes across as an efficient cost-containment machine. The truth is that constraining future health care costs will require a variety of approaches, but in particular it will mean improving the information that providers have about their patients and best practices, and the incentives that providers are given to deliver better care, especially in expensive cases. To lean exclusively or even primarily on shifting costs to consumers would be a mistake.

So here's the message to those vacillating Republican policy makers: There's no need to feel guilty about backing away from the Ryan plan for reasons of political expediency. If your goal is to reduce health spending significantly, you can safely retreat from it on its substance.

Tort Reform Is Needed to Fix Medicare

Richard A. Mathews

Richard A. Mathews is an author and the founder of Voices of United States, a website dedicated to providing education on issues and problems important to the future of the United States.

If you realize the total cost of civil litigation in America annually is basically equal to what we as a nation spent on Medicare/Medicaid in 2007, you can stop reading right now if you wish.

Conversely, if you have never considered the hundreds of billions of dollars each year this country expenses in the costs of civil litigation and the premiums collected to protect both the public and private sector from plaintiff demands, you might wish to continue reviewing this essay.

Updating the Seventh Amendment Guarantee

The Seventh Amendment to our constitution guarantees a civil trial by jury. It does also state,

> "In suits at common law, where the value in controversy shall exceed twenty dollars, the right of trial by jury shall be preserved, and no fact tried by a jury, shall be otherwise re-examined in any court of the United States, than according to the rules of the common law."

This amendment became the law of the land in 1791 when $20 dollars was more than 80% of our citizens earned in a year.

Richard A. Mathews, "Tort Reform Key to Fixing Medicare/Medicaid," *Voices of United States*, August 23, 2011. Voicesof.us. Reproduced by permission.

To gain even more perspective, in 1900—109 years after we established the Bill of Rights—over 80% of the population was considered rural and the median family income stood at $408.

By extension of intent had America revised the 7th Amendment from economic growth in the early part of the 20th century, a trial by Jury would have only been preserved in cases involving at least $400.

Today, according to the U.S. Bureau of Labor and Statistics, the median family income is $52,000.

To bring into perspective the intent of the 7th amendment, our right to a trial by Jury in Civil Court would be guaranteed in any controversy exceeding $50,000.

This is the type of "common sense" change America's Civil Court system desperately needs to have addressed by Federal Legislation.

Contrary to information presented by consumer activist organizations including the ACLU [American Civil Liberties Union, an advocacy group for civil rights] itself, America's Civil Courts system could be made both more cost effective and administer our intended justice for all eliminating a Trial by Jury mandate for litigation under a $50,000 demand.

While there is little information available today on why our founding fathers established a right to Trial by Jury at in excess of $20, there is little doubt that their intent was to insure our citizens were protected by their peers' review of a litigated controversy that could lead to life changing consequences.

What cannot be ignored today are the tens of billions of dollars annually lost from the combination of time Americans spend serving on juries, funds expensed in delays relating to over loaded court dockets and additional insurance premiums collected from both the public and business sector to cover settlements that do not relate to actual economic damages.

I am not contending Tort Reform restrict America's 7th Amendment right to a trial by Jury.

I am contending Tort Reform of the 7th Amendment be updated for 2011 economics.

Limiting Litigation by Medicare/Medicaid Recipients

The second area of Tort Reform America should be considering is our right to litigate due to services rendered by specifically Medicare and Medicaid.

Limiting legal recourse for Medicare and Medicaid recipients to instances of "gross negligence as well as fraud," could annually reduce costs by tens of billions per year.

This area of Tort Reform was debated by both major parties during the development of the American Health Care Act of 2010 [Affordable Care Act or ACA].

It is an area of potential cost savings of such impact, President [Barack] Obama as recently as April of 2011 delivered his support for legislative investigation on the subject.

Depending on which side of this debate you wish to believe, limiting legal recourse for Medicare and Medicaid recipients to instances of "gross negligence as well as fraud," could annually reduce costs by tens of billions per year to as much as a hundred billion annually.

One of the ACA's major cost mitigation components is a program-wide attempt to promote new standards for best practices.

The ACA intends to reward service providers for "best practices," that most cost effectively results in patient recovery both short term and more importantly long term.

This initiative places service providers in a complex decision making arena due to the current limitative environment.

Health care providers who do not follow current standard operational practices leave themselves open to future litigation should a Medicare or Medicaid patient proceed with litigation based on the outcome of their treatment which for multiple reasons they contend is not satisfactory.

Your tax dollars are being spent year in year out defending Medicare and Medicaid health service providers from litigation ranging from replacements of hips using an FDA [US Food and Drug Administration] approved appliance with technically perfect surgery to disfigurement damages from a patient suing for a scar their attorney believes can produce a settlement.

Limiting the right of Medicare/Medicaid patients to litigate would . . . [allow] health care providers to begin the process of putting patient care first without performing every conceivable test.

While there should be no disagreement, a Medicare/ Medicaid patient who receives a hip replacement which is found to be defective has a right to additional surgery, how can America justify paying damages to the patient when the appliance was FDA approved and appropriately installed?

While no citizen should be asked to live with a "disfiguring scar" if it results from improper treatment, how can America justify paying the costs and or settlement damages being awarded in our litigious society?

Only in America can we deem it justice when a woman is awarded a multi-million dollar settlement against McDonald's for spilling hot coffee into her lap while driving?

America is spending roughly $350 Billion per year for the costs associated with its Civil Court system.

That amount is slightly less than our annual national trade deficit and more than the yearly interest cost of the deficit!

Americans'—Your Show Me the Money—mentality has transitioned the civil system from one intended to render justice to one of class warfare by a populous who refuses to accept responsibility for their own choices and actions.

The Need for Tort Reform

Tort reform represents an opportunity to reconnect America with what Thomas Jefferson once noted as the nation's greatest character strength.

"Her right to self-determination, her right to lay the foundations for tomorrow forged from her dreams, hewn from her labor, crafted from her sacrifice, rising forth to create a more bountiful future for herself and her decedents."

Since the establishment of our Bill of Rights, America has preserved her ability to defend the enactment of Justice for all.

Today those same rights need to be updated because of both economic and social conditions which our Founding Fathers could not anticipate in 1791.

Revising our right to trial by Jury to the demand threshold of $50,000 would save the economy over ten billion dollars per year while increasing the efficiency of our court system.

Limiting the right of Medicare/Medicaid patients to litigate would save the economy tens of billions per year while more importantly allowing health care providers to begin the process of putting patient care first without performing every conceivable test available to protect them from future positional liability.

The choice is your America.

The Economics of Financing Medicare

Katherine Baicker and Michael E. Chernew

Katherine Baicker is an economist and a professor of health economics in the Department of Health Policy and Management at the Harvard School of Public Health. Michael E. Chernew is an economist and a professor of health-care policy in the Department of Health Care Policy at Harvard Medical School.

The pressure the Medicare program puts on the federal budget has been much discussed, but financing Medicare also has broader implications for the economy. Medicare expenditures currently account for 15% of federal spending and 3.6% of the total gross domestic product (GDP). Moreover, Medicare spending grew an average of about 2.5 percentage points faster than the GDP from 1976 through 2008, consuming a rapidly increasing share of the country's total resources.

Health care services provided to Medicare beneficiaries are paid for by a combination of dedicated taxes and general revenues—in addition to the care financed by supplemental plans and the 25% of care that beneficiaries pay for through premiums or out of pocket. Medicare Part A (mainly for inpatient expenses) accounts for about 1.7% of the GDP and is largely financed by a dedicated tax on wages (2.9% of earnings, split evenly between workers and their employers but ultimately all coming out of workers' wages). Starting in 2013, high-income workers are scheduled to pay an additional 0.9% tax imposed by the Affordable Care Act (ACA). The payroll taxes are paid into a trust fund, but since 2009 spending has grown more quickly than the revenue stream, and the Part A trust fund is forecast to be exhausted in 2024. At that time, benefits would

Katherine Baicker and Michael E. Chernew, "The Economics of Financing Medicare," *New England Journal of Medicine*, July 28, 2011. NEJM.org. Copyright © 2011 Massachusetts Medical Society. Reproduced by permission.

need to be reduced or other revenue sources found, since there's no provision for filling the projected long-range (75-year) gap between resources coming in and benefits promised (almost 1% of the GDP, under realistic assumptions).

Program costs for Medicare Parts B (physicians and other outpatient care) and D (drugs) are financed mostly through general revenues (about 75%) and beneficiaries' premiums. The cost of these two Medicare components is about 1.9% of the GDP, and it's projected to rise to 3.4% by 2035—even under the improbable assumption that substantial cuts to physician payments under the sustainable growth rate (SGR) formula will be implemented. Since spending on these components of the program is rising rapidly, the share of financing from general revenues is also rising rapidly.

The public financing of Medicare has particular implications for the economy. Specifically, raising taxes to pay for public insurance exerts a structural drag on the economy even if the revenue is spent on care; the same is not true of unsubsidized, privately purchased care of insurance. The net size and timing of the economic consequences depend on how the taxes are raised and how the revenue is spent. Deficit spending on health care also carries an economic cost: taxes are required to pay back any borrowed money (with interest), and rising debt-to-GDP ratios may have calamitous effects on the country's future ability to borrow. Moreover, increased spending on health care is not necessarily good for the economy even if it increases health care employment: spending on low-value health care diverts resources from other uses that could do more to boost the GDP and create jobs.

Although the economy can probably bear some tax increases to help finance Medicare, if recent rates of spending growth continue taxes would have to increase precipitously. An analysis performed by the Congressional Budget Office (CBO) before the ACA was passed suggested that income tax rates would have to increase by more than 70% to finance health care spending that grew just 1 percentage point faster than the GDP—and by more than 160% to finance growth at the historical rate of 2.5 percentage points faster than GDP growth, increasing the income tax rate in the top bracket, for example, to 92% from 35%. Even with just 1 percentage point excess growth in health care spending, the CBO estimates that the tax increase would reduce the GDP by 3 to 16%.

Of course, such tax-financed spending may be worthwhile—the cost of raising the revenue must be weighed against the good done by the program, and Medicare has many costs and benefits beyond its effect on the GDP. Its pooling of risk is crucial to the functioning of insurance markets, if sicker people are disproportionately likely to obtain insurance, premiums will increase, even fewer people will enroll, and insurance markets may eventually collapse. Before Medicare, health insurance was purchased almost exclusively through employers that provided the main source of risk pooling. In 1963, only an estimated 25% of seniors had comprehensive insurance, but shortly after Medicare was created in 1965, virtually all did. The heavy public subsidy of Medicare coverage ensures wide participation and risk pooling.

Although this coverage provides important financial protection and access to care, Medicare's design generates inefficient utilization, which imposes broad indirect costs on all patients. For example, fee-for-service payment discourages coordinated care, and if Medicare benefit or payment design encourages investment in inefficient resources or inefficient care patterns, that can also drive higher and inefficient private spending.

On paper, the ACA significantly reduces the fiscal burden associated with Medicare; the Centers for Medicare and Medicaid Services estimates that it will slow per-beneficiary spending growth to about the rate of GDP growth, largely by reducing payments to providers and health plans. The ACA also establishes pilot mechanisms for transforming fee-for-service

Medicare into a bundled-payment system with broader integration of care, which could promote cost containment by enabling providers to better capture practice efficiencies. Nevertheless, Medicare spending would still consume a growing share of the GDP because of increasing numbers of beneficiaries. Thus, even if the ACA achieves its ambitious goals, Medicare would still need extra resources to solve this demographic problem. Although some additional resources could come from reducing waste in the system, no industrialized country has ever achieved sustained growth rates of health care spending below that of the GDP, so it seems unlikely that Medicare's growth could be reduced below the projected ACA trajectory.

More important, it's unclear how successfully the ACA's fiscal provisions will be implemented. Political will may wane, and the projected savings may not materialize. The use of temporary "patches" to the SGR rather than a longer-term fix illustrates the political challenges involved, and relatively disappointing results from many Medicare demonstration programs illustrate the difficulty of achieving savings.

If the payment-reform and delivery-system strategies in the ACA fall, alternatives will probably involve shifting costs and risk to beneficiaries. One avenue for enacting such a shift would be fixed vouchers (or premium support), which would limit federal liability but, by relying on market mechanisms, place a greater burden on beneficiaries to control spending. The use of market competition is not new: the rationale for the Medicare Advantage (Part C) program included introducing more competition among plans to improve the program's value. Consumers' ability to "discipline the market" depends on the competitiveness of insurers and providers, however, and there is limited evidence that competition among Medicare Advantage plans can sufficiently control spending growth.

Reforms might make competition more effective. For example, competitive pressure might be increased by increasing beneficiaries' incentives to choose low-cost plans, but shifting financial responsibility to beneficiaries can also exacerbate disparities and expose beneficiaries to greater financial risk as health care costs rise relative to their vouchers' value. Or responsibility can be shifted by increasing beneficiaries' cost sharing, a strategy that could discourage the use of lower-value care and limit the program's economic drag—but that must be well designed and operating in a well-regulated environment, particularly if it's to avoid discouraging use of high-value care.

Although Medicare provides invaluable financial protection and access to care for almost 50 million beneficiaries, there's a limit to what we can finance with limited public resources—public programs cannot pay for all possible care for all people. Different plans for limiting Medicare's public resources impose risk on different stakeholders: bundled payments shift financial responsibility and risk to providers; fixed premium support shifts them to beneficiaries. Ultimately, benefit and payment structures must be improved in a clinically informed way that's consistent with high-value care but that also moderates spending growth to keep the program—and the economy—afloat.

Organizations to Contact

The editors have compiled the following list of organizations concerned with the issues debated in this book. The descriptions are derived from materials provided by the organizations. All have publications or information available for interested readers. The list was compiled on the date of publication of the present volume; the information provided here may change. Be aware that many organizations take several weeks or longer to respond to inquiries, so allow as much time as possible.

AARP
601 E St. NW, Washington, DC 20049
(888) 687-2277
website: www.aarp.org

AARP, formerly known as the American Association of Retired Persons, is a nonprofit, nonpartisan membership organization that advocates on behalf of people age fifty and older on issues that affect their independence, health care, and other lifestyle choices. Health care is one of AARP's main priorities, and the group's website contains a wealth of information about Medicare and Medicare reform, much of it located under the Health/Health Insurance and Medicare & Medicaid tab. Examples of publications include: *Understanding Medicare; Closing the "Doughnut Hole" Will Help Protect Over One-Third of Medicare Beneficiaries from High Drug Costs* and *Medicare Premiums in 2012: Better than Expected.*

Centers for Medicare & Medicaid Services (CMS)
7500 Security Blvd., Baltimore, MD 21244
(202) 633-4227
website: www.cms.gov

The Centers for Medicare & Medicaid Services, part of the US Department of Health and Human Services, is a federal agency that runs the Medicare and Medicaid programs. The website provides an overview of the Medicare program as well as a wealth of information about technicalities involved in administration of and compliance with Medicare rules. There is also a newsroom, which is a source of press releases and other information about Medicare changes. CMS also maintains Medicare.gov, an official US government site for Medicare beneficiaries; it contains the latest information on Medicare enrollment, benefits, and other helpful tools.

Doctors for America
1333 H St. NW, 10th Floor, Washington, DC   20005
(202) 481-8219
website: www.drsforamerica.org

Doctors for America is a national grassroots organization of physicians and medical students dedicated to ensuring that everyone has access to affordable, high-quality health care. The group's website contains a section on health-care reform called Learn from the Experts, which features a number of articles on health-care reform and Medicare/Medicaid. Examples include *How to Lower Health Care Costs*, *How Medicare Works and How We Can Improve It*, and *How Medicaid Works and How We Can Improve It*.

Families USA
1201 New York Ave. NW, Suite 1100, Washington, DC   20005
(202) 628-3030 • fax: (202) 347-2417
website: http://familiesusa.org

Families USA is a national, nonprofit, nonpartisan organization dedicated to achieving high-quality, affordable health care for all Americans. The group manages a grassroots advocacy network, acts as a consumer watchdog on issues affecting health care, and produces reports and other information to educate policymakers about the problems facing health-care consumers and how to solve them. Medicare is one of the group's priority issues, and the Families USA website contains a section on this topic, as well as a list of publications. Publications include: *Making the Most of Accountable Care Organi-*

zations (ACOs): What Advocates Need to Know; The Super Committee: Where They Stand on Medicaid, Medicare, and the Affordable Care Act; and *Inside Deficit Reduction: What It Means for Medicare.*

Heritage Foundation

214 Massachusetts Ave. NE, Washington, DC   20002-4999
(202) 546-4400
website: www.heritage.org

The Heritage Foundation is a research and educational institution that proposes and advocates for conservative public policies based on the principles of free enterprise, limited government, individual freedom, traditional American values, and a strong national defense. The foundation's staff conducts research on key policy issues and takes its findings to Congress, congressional staff members, executive branch policymakers, the news media, and academic and policy centers. Health care is one of the group's main issue areas, and its website contains a number of publications on Medicare and Medicare reform. These publications include *How to Fix Medicare: A New Vision for a Better Program, How to Think About Medicare Reform,* and *The First Stage of Medicare Reform: Fixing the Current Program,* among many others.

Henry J. Kaiser Family Foundation

1330 G St. NW, Washington, DC   20005
(202) 347-5270 • fax: (202) 347-5274
website: www.kff.org

The Kaiser Family Foundation is a nonpartisan, nonprofit, private foundation that studies and analyzes major health-care issues facing people in the United States. The group develops and runs its own research and communications programs and serves as a nonpartisan source of facts, information, and analysis for policymakers, the media, the health-care community, and the public. The foundation's website contains information about Medicare. Recent publications include: *Restructuring*

Medicare's Benefit Design: Implications for Beneficiaries and Spending and *Resources on Medicare and the Deficit-Reduction Debate.*

Medicare Rights Center

520 Eighth Ave., North Wing, 3rd Floor, New York, NY   10018
(212) 869-3850 • fax: (212) 869-3532
website: www.medicarerights.org

The Medicare Rights Center is a national, nonprofit, consumer service organization that works to ensure access to affordable health care for older adults and people with disabilities through counseling, advocacy, educational programs, and public policy initiatives. The group helps people understand their Medicare rights and benefits and believes that health care is a basic human right. The center publishes a newsletter, *Medicare Watch*, as well as a variety of other publications on Medicare/Medicaid reform and related issues. Recent examples include *Health Reform and Medicare: The Doughnut Hole in 2012* and *Comments on Eligibility Changes to Medicaid, October 2011.*

National Council on Aging (NCOA)

1901 L St. NW, 4th Floor, Washington, DC   20036
(202) 479-1200
website: www.ncoa.org

The National Council on Aging is a nonprofit service and advocacy organization that acts as a voice for older Americans. Headquartered in Washington, DC, the group works with nonprofit organizations, businesses, and government to develop creative solutions to improve the lives of all older adults. Medicare is one of the issues important to NCOA, and a search of the NCOA website produces a number of informative publications on the topic. Examples include an overview of Medicare, an introduction to Medicare Advantage, and an article titled *Making Sense of Medicare.*

Urban Institute's Health Policy Center
2100 M St. NW, Washington, DC   20037
(202) 833-7200
website: www.urban.org/health_policy/index.cfm

The Urban Institute is an independent, nonpartisan organization that works to create sound public policies and effective government through research, analysis, and education programs. Medicaid is one of the center's major issues, and the organization offers many publications relevant to Medicare reform. Recent publications include: *The Potential Savings from Enhanced Chronic Care Management Policies*; *Improving End-of-Life Care: The English Approach*; *Reducing Unnecessary Hospitalizations of Nursing Home Residents*; *The Role of Prevention in Bending the Cost Curve*; and *Containing the Growth of Spending in the US Health System*.

Bibliography

Books

Henry J. Aaron and Jeanne M. Lambrew	*Reforming Medicare: Options, Tradeoffs, and Opportunities.* Washington, DC: Brookings Institution Press, 2008.
Patricia Barry	*Medicare Prescription Drug Coverage for Dummies.* Hoboken, NJ: For Dummies, 2008.
Charles V. Baylis	*Medicare Advantage: The Alternate Medicare Program.* Hauppauge, NY: Nova Science, 2010.
Daniel Beland and Alex Waddan	*The Politics of Policy Change: Welfare, Medicare, and Social Security Reform in the United States.* Washington, DC: Georgetown University Press, 2012.
Brian D. Boyle et al.	*The Legal Impact of Medicare and Medicaid: Leading Lawyers on the Role of State and Federal Agencies, Effective Compliance Programs, and Enforcement Trends.* Boston, MA: Thomson West/Aspatore Books, 2009.
Robert F. Coulam, Roger Feldman, and Bryan E. Dowd	*Bring Market Prices to Medicare: Essential Reform at a Time of Fiscal Crisis.* Washington, DC: AEI Press, 2009.
Lita Epstein	*The Complete Idiot's Guide to Social Security and Medicare,* 3rd ed. New York: Alpha, 2010.

Roger D. Feldman *How to Fix Medicare: Let's Pay Patients, Not Physicians.* Washington, DC: AEI Press, 2008.

Anthony L. Johnson *Reducing Medicare Fraud, Waste, and Abuse.* Hauppauge, NY: Nova Science, 2011.

Sonya E. King *All About Medicare 2010: Hospital Insurance, Medical Insurance, Prescription Drug Insurance, Medigap, Medicaid.* Erlanger, KY: National Underwriter, 2010.

Frederick R. Lynch *One Nation under AARP: The Fight over Medicare, Social Security, and America's Future.* Berkeley, CA: University of California Press, 2011.

Kimberly J. Morgan and Andrea Louise Campbell *The Delegated Welfare State: Medicare, Markets, and the Governance of Social Policy.* New York: Oxford University Press, 2011.

Leah Rogne et al. *Social Insurance and Social Justice: Social Security, Medicare, and the Campaign Against Entitlements.* New York: Springer, 2009.

Robert E. Stedman *Medicare for Baby Boomers and Beyond.* Salt Lake City, UT: American Book, 2009.

Les Stettner *The War on Medical Terrorism: Why Single-Payer Medicare-for-All Is the Cure for the U.S. Healthcare System.* Bloomington, IN: iUniverse.com, 2009.

US Government Accountability Office	*Medicare Fraud and Abuse: DOJ Has Improved Oversight of False Claims Act Guidance: Report to Congressional Committees.* Memphis, TN: Books LLC, Reference Series, 2011.
Barbara C. Wallace	*Toward Equity in Health: A New Global Approach to Health Disparities.* New York: Springer, 2007.
Alice R. Williamson	*Medicare: A Primer.* Hauppauge, NY: Nova Science, 2010.

Periodicals and Internet Sources

Henry J. Aaron	"The Problems with 'Premium Support' Medicare Reform Plans," *Brookings Up Front Blog*, April 7, 2011. www.brookings.edu.
Todd Ackerman	"Texas Doctors Leaving Medicare Hits Record High," *Houston Chronicle*, March 4, 2011. www.chron.com.
Bruce Bartlett	"The Real Social Security and Medicare Problem (and a Doable Fix)," *New York Times*, May 17, 2011. http://economix.blogs.nytimes.com.
Steve Benen	"Hey, Super-Committee: Here's How to Fix Medicare," *Washington Monthly*, October 25, 2011. www.washingtonmonthly.com.
Robert Bennett	"Medicare Problems Are Many But Solvable," *Deseret News*, May 23, 2011. www.deseretnews.com.

Jose Bidenio   "How to Fix Medicare—Medicare for All," *Daily Kos*, May 27, 2011. www .dailykos.com.

Julie Connelly   "Doctors Are Opting Out of Medicare," *New York Times*, April 1, 2009.

Bob Corker   "How Deficit Committee Should Tackle Medicare," *USA Today*, November 8, 2011.

Kevin Drum   "How Not to Fix Medicare," *Mother Jones*, May 18, 2011. http://mother jones.com.

Kevin Drum   "A Few Little Budget Facts," *Mother Jones*, July 26, 2011. http://mother jones.com.

Chris Farrell   "Medicare Needs a Better Fix than Ryan's," *Business Week*, June 2, 2011. www.businessweek.com.

Margaret Flowers   "Medicare for All Would Save Lives and Money," *The Wichita Eagle*, September 27, 2011. www.kansas .com.

Jeff Goldsmith   "How to Fix Medicare's Doc Fix Problem," *Health Affairs Blog*, January 13, 2011. http://healthaffairs.org.

Scott Hensley   "Study: Doctors More Likely to Drop Private Insurance than Medicare," *NPR*, June 27, 2011. www.npr.org.

Jason Kane   "How Will Debt-Ceiling Deal Affect Medicare for Patients, Doctors?" *PBS Newshour*, August 4, 2011. www.pbs .org.

Kelli Kennedy   "Medicare Fraud: Problems Persist with Contractors Paid Millions to Ferret Out Bogus Bills," *Huffington Post*, November 14, 2011. www .huffingtonpost.com.

Andrew Leonard   "The Smart Way to Fix Medicare: Healthcare Reform," *Salon*, August 20, 2010. www.salon.com.

Robert Moffit and James C. Capretta   "How to Fix Medicare: A New Vision for a Better Program," Heritage Foundation, December 13, 2010. www.heritage.org.

Robert Moffit, Gail Wilensky, and James Capretta   "How Should Washington Control Medicare Spending?" Heritage Foundation, August 30, 2011. www.heritage.org.

Robert Pear   "Rise in Medicare Premium Is Lower than Predicted," *New York Times*, October 27, 2011.

Pat Regnier   "What No One Is Telling You About Medicare," *Money*, October 21, 2011. http://money.cnn.com.

Kate Santich   "As More Use Hospice, Medicare Sees Sharp Rise in Costs, Problems," *Orlando Sentinel*, October 29, 2011. http://articles.orlandosentinel.com.

US Department
of Health and
Human Services

"Affordable Care Act to Help
Improve Care for Medicare
Beneficiaries," October 24, 2011.
www.hhs.gov.

David Whelen

"10 Reasons the Deficit Super
Committee Should Cut Medicare,"
Forbes, November 1, 2011.
www.forbes.com.

Index

A

B

C